A PRIMER ON BROWNING

A PRIMER

ON

BROWNING

BY

F. MARY WILSON

KENNIKAT PRESS
Port Washington, N. Y./London

A PRIMER ON BROWNING

First published in 1891
Reissued in 1970 by Kennikat Press
Library of Congress Catalog Card No: 72-113351
ISBN 0-8046-1039-8

Manufactured by Taylor Publishing Company   Dallas, Texas

CONTENTS.

CHAPTER I.

BROWNING'S LITERARY LIFE.

		PAGE
1.	'Lives of the Poets'	1
2.	Browning's Reticence and Openness	2
3.	Parentage	3
4.	Childhood and Education	5
5.	Earlier Manhood	6
6.	Marriage and Middle Life	9
7.	Later Life	10

CHAPTER II.

BROWNING'S CHARACTERISTICS.

1.	Universality	15
2.	Courage	16
3.	Philosophy and Religion	17

CONTENTS.

	PAGE
4. Subjects	23
5. The Art of Browning	36
6. Browning as a Writer of Plays	41
7. Defects and Difficulties	43

CHAPTER III.

INTRODUCTIONS TO THE POEMS.

Pauline	49
Paracelsus	53
Strafford	61
Sordello	64
Pippa Passes	75
King Victor and King Charles	78
Dramatic Lyrics	81
The Return of the Druses	83
A Blot in the 'Scutcheon	86
Colombe's Birthday	88
Dramatic Romances and Lyrics	92
Luria	97
A Soul's Tragedy	101
Christmas-Eve and Easter-Day	103
Men and Women	108
Dramatis Personæ	124
The Ring and the Book	131

CONTENTS.

	PAGE
Balaustion's Adventure	161
Prince Hohenstiel-Schwangau	166
Fifine at the Fair	170
Red Cotton Night-Cap Country	177
Aristophanes' Apology	182
The Inn Album	188
Pacchiarotto and how he Worked in Distemper: with other Poems	196
The Agamemnon of Æschylus	202
La Saisiaz: The Two Poets of Croisic	207
Dramatic Idyls	211
Jocoseria	220
Ferishtah's Fancies	226
Parleyings with Certain People	233
Asolando	239
Index	246

N.B.—The references to the Poems, by page, are to *The Poetical Works of Robert Browning*, Smith, Elder, 1888, in sixteen volumes; and to *Asolando*, Smith, Elder, 1890.

A PRIMER ON BROWNING.

CHAPTER I.

BROWNING'S LITERARY LIFE.

1. 'Lives of the Poets.'—A great writer's life is to be found in his works rather than in his biography. The essential life of Wordsworth, George Eliot, and Carlyle is absorbed in their writings, and any other record of their years is comparatively fruitless lore. Out of the raw material of their sensations and perceptions they weave a finished product, with which alone we need greatly concern ourselves. The necessity to specialise and subdivide various departments of human labour increases with each century, and men who are at once famous as warriors, courtiers, statesmen, and poets scarcely exist in our times. Even a master spirit now has to exert himself to the utmost before he can make a step in advance of all that has already been created or discovered in one field alone.[1] Accordingly the observers and transcribers of life tend more and more to become a

[1] Works, XII. 89. *Red Cotton Night-Cap Country.*

separate class, so that the lives of the literary men of this age are, to speak broadly, private and uneventful.

2. **Browning's Reticence and Openness.**—Having allowed all this, it is still natural that we should wish to know something of what were the makings of a great poet as we read him in his works, and in what circumstances the works were written. Some outline of such facts is precious, for often what specially hallows our poets to us is a silent happiness or fortitude of living which no reader's spirit-sense could unaided find between the lines. The more dramatic a writer is, the less easy it is to construct his personality out of his writings, and no writer ever had a more dramatic spirit running through his poems than Browning. If we read *Childe Harold* or *Elia* we lay them down with some idea of what manner of men were Byron and Lamb, but it is Browning's ideal[1] and his individual claim,[2] that through the poet's 'window' all men may look, but no foot be allowed across his 'threshold.' Moreover, Browning's poetical works fill at least seventeen volumes, and are, as has been said, not books but a literature. Yet no one who studies these seventeen volumes fails to find the presentation of a personality subdominant throughout, a personality more explicit, it may be, in one place than another, and only speaking with direct utterance in some later poems entirely, and elsewhere in

[1] XIII. 40, 41. *Aristophanes' Apology.*
[2] XIV. 39. *House.*

scattered passages, but always the same Browning, self-expressed, even when most dramatic, in his selection of characters and their action, one whose moral tests and spiritual hopes, hatreds, loves, and scorns are (even in his own despite, if that be so) ours to know. Most minds possess marked opposites of their strongest characteristics, and so Browning's professed austerity of attitude [1] towards his readers is at most the reaction from that great instinct of self-revealing which he shares with every other poet.

3. **Parentage.**—Robert Browning was born May 7th, 1812. His father, also Robert, for nearly fifty years a clerk in the Bank of England, was the son of another Robert Browning, who held an important post in the same place for over the half century. The Brownings had been Dorsetshire people, but London and the West of England did not supply the only pre-natal streams that flowed into the blood of the poet. It is extremely interesting to know, as any observer of his sympathies and insights would reasonably expect, that he came of mixed nationalities. His grandmother on the paternal side was a Creole, owning a sugar plantation at St. Kitt's, where his father spent some time when a youth. His mother, Sarianna Wiedemann, born at her parents' home in Dundee, was the daughter of a mother who was pure Scots and a father of German extraction. There is no proof, though the question has been mooted, that

[1] XIV. 31. *At the "Mermaid."* XV. 164. Epilogue to *Dramatic Idyls.* XVI. 89. Lyric to *A Bean-Stripe, Ferishtah's Fancies.*

this grandfather on the spindle side had any Jewish traces.

Thus there were in Browning mingled threads of nationality, worked upon a web of English middle class. In Browning's heredity were germinated his vast intellectual and emotional range and his susceptibility to race differences, but the genius which modulated these varying strains into undreamed-of harmony was his own. As we shall see, intelligence and cultivation were preparing in the Browning family before 1812, but though something of the perfected intelligence we call genius may be prepared by progenitors, much more seems directly inspired by the breath of a wind which bloweth where it listeth.[1]

Browning's grandfather was an expert man of business. His father was a genial, popular man, versatile and accomplished. Besides his clever caricatures of faces, well known in the Bank of England, he was learned in art history. He could improvise and illustrate stories in rhyme for the children. He "was a scholar and knew Greek,"[2] and used to rock his little boy in his arms to the sound of Anacreon. In English poetry he adhered to Pope's secure couplets, in contradistinction to his wife, who liked more innovating fashions of verse. Both parents were Congregationalists. One of the poet's uncles, William Shergold Browning, wrote a highly regarded *History*

---

[1] See, on this subject, XI. 202, 203.
[2] *Asolando.* 123. *Development.*

of the Huguenots. An interesting note on Browning's father is his ingenuity in the dovetailing of detective evidence, and his intimacy with mediæval legends, "he seemed to have known Paracelsus and even Talmudic personages personally," a noteworthy environment for the future author of *The Ring and the Book, Pietro of Abano, Paracelsus,* and *Jochanan Hakkadosh.* Doubtless Browning's inherited vigour and buoyancy of constitution helped to preserve his cheerful trust in unprovable spiritualities from the falterings and backslidings of other men. What of the poet's mother? She was a religious woman who loved music, and whom her son loved with never-forgetting emotion.

4. **Childhood and Education.**—Browning was born in Southampton Street, Peckham. That suburb and its neighbours, Camberwell and Herne Hill, were less absorbed then than now into the circle of fog and soot, and we may think of Browning's childhood as spent among 'old trees,' 'climbing plants,' and 'morning swallows.'[1] His imagination was deeply impressed by distant London, murmurous, lighting the sky by night, and imaging that 'need of a world of men'[2] so paramount in the after years. We hear of Avison's March, to the air of which the little boy would step,[3] of an Italian engraving of Andromeda,[4] of the tale of Troy as

---

[1] I. 8. *Pauline.*
[2] VI. 46. *Parting at Morning.*
[3] XVI. 223. *Parleyings. With Charles Avison.*
[4] I. 29. *Pauline.*

suggested by the outlines of the coals in the grate. Such trifles fed his fancy-hunger. Some of the poems of Browning's maturity drew their magic suggestion from isolated memories of childhood, and a habit of seeing human contours in coals and clouds may have originated such a memorable tableau of the sunset's Persian encounter as we find in *Gerard de Lairesse* in *Parleyings*.

Till he was fourteen, Browning was taught at private schools near home. Then he studied for a time with a tutor, who used to come to his father's house. When, in 1829, University College, London, was opened, Browning attended a few lectures there. The bald enumeration of such chartered means of education seems in Browning's case peculiarly vain. Browning's are the works of a great reader, a winner of universal knowledge, and he early began to assimilate his proper food. His brief inthralment to Byron, of which boyish verses were the natural acknowledgment, was annulled, in 1826, by a wondrous boon, for then Browning became possessed of the poems of Shelley and Keats. It was a memorable day to the coming poet when the inspiring beauty of those earlier twain was revealed to him.

5. **Earlier Manhood.**—His son and daughter having the prospect of fair means, there was wisely no thought with Browning's father of tying Robert down to uncongenial occupation to make money withal. Browning was left free to follow his own bent, *i.e.* to make poetry his profession.

LITERARY LIFE.

In 1832, Browning wrote *Pauline*, and in 1833 it was published. Soon after this, the poet went abroad for nearly a year. Travel was a valuable element in the shaping of Browning. He went to Russia, and Italy, first visited in 1838, was, in his own phrase, his 'University.' He delved into the history, famous and out-of-the-way, of the places he stayed in,[1] and became familiar with the people. In the Italian journey of 1838, he made his first acquaintance with his perennial loves, Asolo[2] and Venice.[3]

In 1835, *Paracelsus*, Browning's first acknowledged work, was published, and about the same time several brilliant and spirited short poems came out in the *Monthly Repository*, which was edited by Browning's firm friend, Mr. W. Johnson Fox. Among these were the two, *Johannes Agricola* and *Porphyria* (called later *Porphyria's Lover*), which, in 1842, were combined under the title of *Madhouse Cells*. Many of Browning's earlier friendships, with the great men who belonged to the generation that was old when he himself was young, date from the appearance of *Paracelsus*.

At Macready's instance, Browning wrote a tragedy, and *Strafford* was produced at Covent Garden Theatre, May 1st, 1837. The drama, like much of *Paracelsus*, had been partly conceived during those midnight walks, dear to the imagination of Browning, in a wood near Dulwich. The play was not unsuccessful, but it was more than the most successful play could

---

[1] I. 285, 286. *Sordello*.   [2] I. 159. *Sordello*.
[3] I. 161. *Sordello*.

do to prop the tottering fortunes of Covent Garden Theatre. After five nights the financial storm broke, and *Strafford* bent to it. As Browning's boyish writings had been considered too easily melodious and transparent, so *Paracelsus* was condemned by Sterling and Caroline Fox for being verbose. Browning laid the unexpected word to heart, and *Sordello* (1840) witnesses to its bitter fruit, for the music of *Pauline* and *Paracelsus* is silenced, and in one word he essays the work of five. *Strafford* is concise too, not with the curtailed compressions of *Sordello*, but only in keeping with the stern conciseness of its chronicle and characters. *Sordello* was attacked and ridiculed on all sides, and from this time forth Browning followed his own course and took no more lessons from his critics.[1] He had to work and wait for two more decades before any full measure of public recognition became his. As we can well imagine, such neglect was disadvantageous to his art and bitter and hard to bear. In the years following on *Strafford*, Browning wrote a number of poetical dramas. Two of these, *A Blot in the 'Scutcheon* and *Colombe's Birthday*, were performed in by the chief actors of the time—Macready, Miss Helena Faucit, and Phelps. The plays, together with many short poems, included in later editions under the headings of *Dramatic Lyrics*, *Dramatic Romances*, and *Men and Women*, came out, between 1841 and 1846, in eight

---

[1] XIII. 70, 71. *Aristophanes' Apology*; XVI. 257. *The Two Poets of Croisic*; and XV. 260. *Pambo*.

numbers, bearing the general name of *Bells and Pomegranates*. This name, borrowed from the decoration round the high-priest's robe, was thus explained by Browning,[1] "I meant by the title to indicate an endeavour towards something like an alternation, or mixture of music with discoursing, sound with sense, poetry with thought, which looks too ambitious thus expressed, so the symbol was preferred." Browning's taste was ever towards such symbols, imaginatively beautiful in themselves, nor was it always his first care to point out how they should be read. First in the series of *Bells and Pomegranates* was that wonderful *proverbe*, *Pippa Passes* (1841).

6. **Marriage and Middle Life.**—The forties form a great epoch in the story of Robert Browning, not only for the marvellous poems he was then writing, but for the commencement of a perfect inward poem, his marriage with Elizabeth Barrett, which took place September 12th, 1846. A week later, the two poets left England, and Mrs. Browning's health for ever forbade her return on any but flitting visits. The first winter was spent in Pisa, the summer in Ancona and its neighbourhood. Before the next winter Mr. and Mrs. Browning had taken up their residence in Florence. Except the house of the Alighieri, there is no spot in Florence so sacred for poetry's sake as Casa Guidi. Here, on March 9th, 1849, a child, Robert Wiedemann Barrett Browning, was born. The Brownings spent two or three of their winters in Rome, and one in

[1] (No. VIII.) Preface to *A Soul's Tragedy*.

Paris with Mr. Browning's father and sister, who were living there. Florence gave Browning the prompting idea of his famous Art poems, such as *Andrea del Sarto*. The time was rich in poetic plans formed and carried out. Mrs. Browning wrote *Casa Guidi Windows*, *Aurora Leigh*, and other famous poems, and the publication of the fifty—and One—*Men and Women*, in 1855, marks a new era in the widening renown of Browning. In 1861, the golden union underwent the sorrow that comes to all unions, for, on June 29th, the fragile life of Mrs. Browning passed beyond mortal ken. A few months after, Browning wrote *Prospice*, that grand testimony to the faith that looks through death. Three years after, the poem was published in *Dramatis Personæ*. In 1868-69 Browning's giant work, *The Ring and the Book*, was given to the world. At the beginning of it, Browning tells how, in 1865, he accidentally picked up, at a book-stall in Florence, the square, yellow book, the record of the Franceschini trial, that was the germ of his wonderful production.

7. **Later Life.**—Bereft of his Wife, Browning ceased to consider Italy his home, and with his boy he came to live in London, at 19. Warwick Crescent, like the Valladolid poet's, a 'stuccoed third house by the bridge.'[1] After the death of their father, in 1866, his sister, Miss Browning, came to live with him, and continued to do so till he died. From 1868 forward, few were the years unmarked by a book by Brown-

[1] IV. 179. *How it Strikes a Contemporary*.

LITERARY LIFE.

ing. In 1887, Browning left Paddington for 29. De Vere Gardens. He went abroad every year, and *Red Cotton Night-Cap Country*, *La Saisiaz*, and *Asolando* record such visits. Browning spent his autumns in Venice.

In *The Flight of the Duchess*, Browning wrote:

"What a thing friendship is, world without end!"[1]

and no man has lived his life through more encompassed with friends. The only ones of whom it behoves here to speak are those to whom Browning refers in his works. We remember how Meres spoke of Shakspere's 'sugred sonnets among his private friends,' and the same epithet applies to Browning's dedications. Among the loved and loving friends in Browning's poems, we early find the names of John Forster and M. Milsand of Dijon,[2] the French critic, and Browning's enthusiastic admirer. Walter Savage Landor is referred to in *Sordello*,[3] and *Luria* is dedicated to him. Browning's goodness to Landor, when the older poet stood in urgent need of a friend's help, is one of the many lovable traits of his character. 'My English Eyebright' of the third Book of *Sordello*[4] is Miss Euphrasia Haworth, an early friend. *Paracelsus* is inscribed to another, Count de Ripert-Monclar, and *Strafford* to William Macready, for whose little boy, Willy, Browning wrote the *Pied Piper*, not thinking at the time of including it among

[1] V. 150.
[2] It was the 1863 reprint of *Sordello* that was dedicated to M. Milsand.
[3] I. 169-170.
[4] I. 170.

his 'works.' In three epigrammatic lines, Browning dedicated *Pippa Passes* to Mr. Sergeant Talfourd, and the literary name of Procter is affectionately written at the beginning of *Colombe's Birthday*. To John Kenyon, Miss Barrett's cousin, who introduced the poet and poetess to each other, and possessed social and intellectual eminence as well as wealth and generosity, Browning dedicated *Dramatic Lyrics* (1842). The original of 'Waring' was Mr. Domett, a lyrical writer, sometime a minister of state in New Zealand, and the 'Alfred' to whom *The Guardian-Angel* is addressed. Belonging to Browning's later period (*i.e.* taking *The Ring and the Book*, 1868-69), as in some sort a boundary between the first and second halves of Browning's literary life) is the charming inscription of *Balaustion's Adventure* to Lady Cowper, who had inspired its production. Browning dedicated his selection from his poetry (1872) to Tennyson, to whom, in the preface to an earlier nosegay (1865), he had done graceful homage. *Red Cotton Night-Cap Country*, besides being formally 'to Miss Thackeray,' is full of sweet and informal reference to her and to honoured Milsand. In the prose 'chat,' that goes with the *Agamemnon*, Browning quotes from one 'eloquent friend,' Matthew Arnold, and refers his own work to another, 'dear and noble,' Carlyle. The subject of Browning's '*In Memoriam*,' *La Saisiaz*, is Miss Anne Egerton Smith. *Parleyings* is sacred to the memory of the highly valued Joseph Milsand. With *Asolando* goes a letter to Mrs. Bronson, Browning's

American friend and hostess at Venice and Asolo. 'My Kirkup,' who appears in a parenthesis on the first page of *Pacchiarotto*, was a Florentine acquaintance, the discoverer of Giotto's portrait of Dante in the Bargello. John Relfe, apostrophised in *Charles Avison*, had been one of Browning's music-masters in boyhood.

In 1872, Browning's popularity was proved and furthered by the issue of two volumes in the Tauchnitz edition of poems selected from his works. Browning was made Honorary Fellow of Balliol in 1868, and honorary degrees have been given him by Oxford, Cambridge, and Edinburgh. Browning took great pride in his artist son, and that son's marriage to an American lady, Miss Fanny Coddington, meant yet another affectionate bond to the old man. Browning, by character and career, stands among the sane and well-ordered representatives of a high civilisation, which allows of 'placid lives, leisurely works.'[1] It was a part of his transcendentalism to insist that the soul, instead of aging like the body, grows and gains,[2] and certainly he lived out his own belief. The last works of 'Rabbi' Browning are mellow, and have none of the spleen of advanced years. Browning had not learnt from his Greeks their cruel worship of youth and abhorrence of age.[3] In the passage[4] in *Aristophanes' Apology* in which Aristo-

---

[1] XIV. 239. *The Two Poets of Croisic.*
[2] XI. 245. *Fifine at the Fair.*
[3] XIII. 272. *Agamemnon.* [4] XIII. 40, 41.

phanes depicts a poet in and out of the world, there seems a likeness to the poet who was so fond of, and yet so independent of society, able to dispense himself prodigally because conscious of the colossal strength which he had only to shut his study door upon the silken company to renew. Browning's personal appearance was expressive to those who could see deep enough. His eyes wonderfully combined searching scrutiny with the meditative far-off regard. Landor, long ago describing Browning's exterior personality, spoke of the spruce, hale man, with 'active step,' 'inquiring eye,' and 'tongue so varied in discourse.'

In the autumn of 1889, after spending some time at Asolo, Browning moved on to Venice, to the Rezzonico Palace, the property of his daughter and son. There, late in November, he was attacked by bronchitis, aggravated by asthma, and rendered serious by weak action of the heart. On December 12th, after a short illness, he died at the age of seventy-seven.

It was thought that what was mortal of the poet would lie by his wife in the Florentine cemetery, but this was not to be. England claimed her poet for Westminster Abbey. On December 31st, 1889, the body of Browning was interred in Poets' Corner, amid a great throng of witnesses, representative of England's best.

CHAPTER II.

BROWNING'S CHARACTERISTICS.

1. **Universality.**—No criticism on Browning has surpassed those lines written by his wife, then Miss Barrett, wherein she individualised him by his 'veined humanity," and added that his works, 'pomegranates' indeed, need cutting deep to come at the red heart within. The greatest passion and the utmost power of Browning are spent in depicting men and women. His poems are full of incidents; he ransacks history and the world for curious and effective stories; but to Browning, unlike Scott or Homer, incident alone is meaningless, valuable only as an opportunity for revealing character. Browning is most at home with complexity, outward and inward. The more exceptional the incident, the more exceptional and interesting the character, according to him. That is why his works are so full, and ever increasingly so, of the out-of-the-way, occasionally the repellent. With every poet matter and manner are wedded, and with none more indissolubly than with Browning. Every thing in Browning, his ideas, especially those which at first seem contradictory, his beliefs, his selection of subjects, his defects and untowardnesses prove on close inspection to be parts of the most immutable, welded whole. His continuous unity of thought and purpose is extraordinary.

Browning's penetrative sympathy delights to enter all the various forms of life, to try to look through each man's eyes, and describe in his character how his outside world is affecting the individual within. In Browning's harvesting all ranks afford an equally rich yield of humanity. He shows the husk, only to remove it and present us with the soul. He is as interested in psychologising a Paris jeweller as a queen. The soul in each is his great object of study, the soul testing itself on circumstances,[1] strong if it aims, grows, fights on,[2] despicable if it shirks conflict.[3]

2. **Courage.**—In nothing is Browning more remarkable than in the second light he will throw on actions and motives, and in his new treatment of old episodes. After every one else has comfortably acquiesced in some 'obvious' verdict and fancied that further appeal is over, how poor and crude that verdict appears under the illumination of this mind, late in time, but fresh as the primal morning! Take, for instance, in *The Ring and the Book*, the unconventional summing-up of the Pope on Guido, with that sublime illustrative storm,[4] only excelled by the matchless tempest in *Pippa Passes*.[5] The same electric light flashes out in *Iván Ivánovitch*, in the old priest's judgment, swift and

---

[1] VII. *Rabbi ben Ezra. Et passim.*
[2] IV. 266. *Bishop Blougram's Apology.*
[3] V. *The Statue and the Bust.*
[4] X. 147, 148. *The Ring and the Book. The Pope.*
[5] III. 23. *Pippa Passes. Morning.*

overturning as one of Christ's.[1] Similar originality and fearlessness come out in *The Glove* and *Clive*. Then what an unusual view of death there is in *Prospice*! Browning ever sides with the fighter, eager 'to grapple danger whereby souls grow strong,'[2] as in his view of temptation, which he would wish to have dragged up by its hair in order to do battle with it.[3] The second light he throws on character appears in his reasoning too, as in the opulent re-inforcement in *Two Camels*[4] to the argument against asceticism. A curious extra argument, entirely Browning's own, is to be found in *Fifine at the Fair*, XI. cxxviii. Another instance occurs in Fust's dilemma of conscience in the *Epilogue* to *Parleyings*.[5] There is not one line of fluff or claptrap in Browning.

3. **Philosophy and Religion.**—Browning is not solely a poetic artist, he is besides that a 'thinker,' with so persistent an answer to the ultimate question of life that few of his poems can be appraised without reference to it. He would have thought his work of little worth if it only served to mirror the chance and scattered experience of many men, or give artistic satisfaction by its mere perfection of utterance. If he did not originate the broadest expression of nineteenth century belief, at least he transmutes it, so that through his poetry it re-enters many a soul

---

[1] XV. 50-54. *Iván Ivánovitch*.
[2] X. 116. *The Pope*, line 1302.
[3] X. 111. *The Pope*, lines 1185-1192.
[4] XVI. 49, 50.   [5] XVI. 252, 273-274.

with healing in its wings. To many people his works are a latter evangel of reasonable Christianity. Browning restates, in language proper to our day, the need, the fitness, one might say the inevitableness of two correlative beings, the soul and God. While he acknowledges that these two existences are unprovable, being beyond the region of scientific experiment, he, for his own part, takes them as self-evident and the 'knowledge' of them as intuitive. Like Wordsworth, he looks within, not without, for the sources of knowledge.[1] Knowledge from within he deems absolute truth and, at the same time, transcendent mystery. The existence of the soul is the root of Browning's philosophy, the one thing in it which is taken for granted. The soul being allowed as the subject—that which perceives, that which is perceived—God, follows as a matter of course, the object complementary to the subject. Browning has a fine passage in *Red Cotton Night-Cap Country* in which he definitely confronts the insidious idea of soul and body being one and the same, 'the new *Religio Medici*,' as he calls it,[2] and there he explains his own concept of body, as ministrant and servant to soul, not including soul in itself. To recapitulate:—the soul represents to Browning the fundamental fact of life, it is the basis of his philosophy, and the only part of it which transcends logical proof. In every further step Browning

---

[1] XV. 243. *Jochanan Hakkadosh.*
[2] XII. 113. *Red Cotton Night-Cap Country.*

addresses himself to the intellect and submits his arguments to its severest tests. While his process is intellectual, it is far from being colourless. A philosopher, dealing with abstract ideas, appeals solely to intellect, so does a historian, discussing the value of documentary evidence, but Browning is above every thing a poet, and a poet ascribing the deepest thrill of his inspiration to a religion which represents the vitalising and personal element in philosophy and history. Both the man and the theme are in touch with the heart and the emotions. Herein lies the value to religion of a great poet when enlisted in its service, he above all men having the faculty for raising the key of the appeal so that it enters the soul by the double gateway of intellect and feelings. There is something very sustaining to weaker faith in the unfaltering vigour of Browning's. One of the greatest intellects of the age encounters materialistic thought with a constant determination to 'hope hard in the subtle thing that's spirit.'[1] In the very uncertainty of the unseen, Browning finds the foremost evidence of its truth. Life is probation, the race-ground of the soul, and souls develop only when will and faith have perfectly free play.[2] He never tires of stating and exemplifying this cardinal idea, he looks at it from every side, and never finds it fail. In *Fears and Scruples* we have one of his strangest illustrations of the spiritual

[1] XIV. 4. *Prologue* to *Pacchiarotto*.
[2] IV. 191, 192. *An Epistle*.

uses of uncertainty. The existence of evil offers development to man's moral energy, just as the noblest possibility of human love is provided for by the existence of pain and weakness.[1] Our failures are an evidence of our ultimate triumph, and life's shortness and imperfection imply immortality. Browning is Wagner in literature; for both, discords exist to be quenched in concord.[2]

Given God's power and knowledge, His love is as inevitable as the third angle of the triangle. Man's sublimest love being the strength of weakness, Browning sees nothing for it but that God's love should be similar in manifestation. This is the point at which he is touched by the appeal of Christ.[3] God's love once proved a necessity, no way lies open by which it can meet man half-way but by clothing its strength in weakness like man's own. How can man bridge the gulf between his own need and the claim Christ made? Shall he 'reject Christ through very need of Him'?[4] No, for Christianity is the only hypothesis by which Browning, and those who have been able to follow him thus far, can 'solve all questions in the earth and out of it,'[5] even while taking every opposing difficulty into consideration.

To Browning all secondary dogma is subject to the relativity of truth. Man's knowledge and condi-

[1] VI. 117. *Saul,* and XIV. *La Saisiaz.*
[2] VII. 108. *Abt Vogler,* and XVI. 224. *With Charles Avison.*
[3] VI. 122. *Saul,* and XVI. 30. *Ferishtah: The Sun.*
[4] VII. 141. *A Death in the Desert.*
[5] VII. 139. *A Death in the Desert.*

tions suit his degree of development. He is accorded just so much truth as will prick him on to earn more. Education comes to the race, as to every child,[1] by gradual steps, by concessions to weakness and ignorance, by a slowly increasing grant of opportunities to develop and leave childish horizons and old illusions, *i.e.* old aids, behind. "Law deals the same with soul and body."[2] Browning affirms the existence of 'a falsish false' and 'a falsish true,'[3] as well as truth pure and simple, the difference between them being that the falsity is fleeting, a means to the end, which is truth itself.[4] Delusions are essential to man's growth, and whom God deludes, Browning considers well deluded.

" When faith is ripe for sight,—why, reasonably then
Comes the great clearing-up. Wait threescore years and ten!"

Browning's ever present thought is the individual soul as judged individually.[5] He constantly reiterates the independent personal relation that exists between the soul and God. While he believes that every man shall give account of his own soul first and foremost, he thinks no less of the other side of the shield, the working out, or rather the witness, of soul in love and sacrifice. He never tires of saying, "Love is best," "Love is all and Death is nought," "Renounce

[1] *Asolando*, p. 123. *Development*, and VII. 115. *Rabbi Ben Ezra*.
[2] XVI. 118. *Parleyings, Bernard de Mandeville*.
[3] XII. 65. *Red Cotton Night-Cap Country*.
[4] XI. 332, 333. *Fifine at the Fair*.
[5] V. 291, 292. *Christmas-Eve and Easter-Day*, VII. 254, *Epilogue*, and XVI. 72, *Ferishtah's Fancies: A Bean-Stripe*.

joy for my fellows' sake ? That's joy beyond joy."
The question Browning would ask at the end of any
man's life is not, What has he done ? but, What did he
try to do ? Other lives may follow this, let them suffice
for perfection, all man can do here is to tend upward.
If his reach be beyond his grasp, so much the better,
therein lies his warrant of immortality. A comparison between the spirituality of Browning and
that of Lord Tennyson is suggested by the conclusion of *Apparent Failure*, which closely resembles
much in *In Memoriam*. Generally speaking, where
Lord Tennyson is meditative, Browning is argumentative, showing us his thought in process as it moves
from point to point. In this, the difference between
the two poets resembles the similar difference between
S. John and S. Paul. But while Browning delights in
demonstrating the entire structure of his belief, Lord
Tennyson's belief is a sentiment, a pensive desire, a
temperamental bias, shaken by materialistic thought.
Though Browning weaves in the ideas, terms, and
tales of science as much as does his great compeer,
he is far less affected by its pessimism. He is really
disregardful of it, being principally occupied with the
spiritual region which science ignores. There is no record in Browning's work of a personally sceptical stage.
Even *Pauline*, far from being touched with a young
man's infidelity, such as finds extreme expression in
Shelley's earlier work, is markedly religious, even
devout. Dramatically, of course, as in *Christmas-Eve
and Easter-Day*, Browning frequently travels over the

waste places in which he himself seems never to have lingered. His imagination loves the larger possibilities offered it by faith. Yet the optimism of his watchword, "Trust God nor be afraid," is not really easy-going. Such a charge is effectually replied to in *Red Cotton Night - Cap Country*, cxxviii. Equally significant as a reply is Browning's comparison of faith to the angel Michael, with the snake, unbelief, beneath his foot, treading firmer, "because he feels it writhe."[1] Browning is a later Coleridge, with a theological instinct less bounded and more acute than Coleridge's, manageable, not nebulous, thinking about men, not about thought. In another direction, some readers are disappointed to find certain characters, as in *The Pope and the Net*, dismissed without blame or punishment. Browning sympathises with energy of life, with life as life, and, keenly aware of life's complexity, he cannot constrain it or dogmatise about it in any narrow or restricted way. If he occasionally troubles us by his seeming sympathy with evil and mischief, it is of his dramatic imagination, like the Shaksperian artistry which joyed equally in presenting Iago and Desdemona. There is room in a great master for many theories, without his being himself bounded by any, nor is the consistency of Browning's philosophy marred, but rather strengthened, by his sufferance of evil.

4. **Subjects.**—Browning cares far more for the individual than for men in masses. Unlike Shak-

[1] IV. 265. *Bishop Blougram's Apology.*

spere, he troubles little about national life. He shows a growing[1] indifference, which is half scorn, for general movements. The collective progress of the race and the material advancement of civilisation do not swell his theme as they do Lord Tennyson's, or intoxicate him as they do Whitman. In this regard, a Wordsworthian aloofness characterises Browning. Indeed, Browning is in saneness and tonic effect, and also, it must be said, in a tendency to prolixity, Wordsworth's lineal descendant. The blazing questions of the day all seem to Browning to be more or less beside the mark. 'Prince Hohenstiel-Schwangau' (XI. 162, 163) compares the socialistic and individualistic views to the disadvantage of the former, and in *Pacchiarotto* Browning laughs at socialists' belief that 'aims heavenly' can be 'attained by means earthly.' He rejoices in the impossibility, since he sees imperfection necessary to the world, and only personal reform valuable. His favourite 'revolutionary' is sober Pym. Browning's reply[2] to his question, "How can I help England?"[3] is not concerned with democratic solutions. Like Chaucer, like Shakspere, though perhaps from different causes, he does not love the mob. There is very little of the fanatic or the enthusiast about him. Responsibility and retribution are his leading notes. He believes in 'war for hate of war,'[4] he glories in the failure of science to explain

[1] Compare II. 36, 171. *Paracelsus* with XV. 242. *Jochanan Hakkadosh.*   [2] XIV. 203. *La Saisiaz.*
[3] VI. 97. *Home-Thoughts, from the Sea.*
[4] XI. 200. *Prince Hohenstiel-Schwangau.*

the facts of heredity,[1] he upholds the punishment of death,[2] finding in his Æschylus that blood is the inevitable price of blood,[3] that "the killer has all to pay."

Against Vivisection Browning has directed two poems, *Tray* and *Arcades Ambo*. Similar in application are *Donald* and *The Lady and the Painter*. The other Animal Poems are *How they brought the Good News* and *Muléykeh*. Browning is always ready to speak for the speechless, and his references to animals are as observant as they are sympathetic. The idea of the hero, even a dog hero,[4] is characteristic of him.

Concerning children (with the exception of *The Pied Piper of Hamelin*, which was written expressly for a child), and the parental and filial relation, Browning has few specific poems. Pompilia's motherhood,[5] in *The Ring and the Book*, is unsurpassed in our literature. Pompilia, with her babe, reflects the white and tender holiness of a Rafael Madonna. In *Iván Ivánovitch*, Browning speaks his mind on parental responsibility and the sacredness of motherhood, of which Dmītri's wife is the disgrace, as Pompilia is the exquisite example. "Womanliness means only motherhood," Browning says in *The Inn Album*.[6] *Halbert and Hob* is the story of the terrible savagery

---

[1] XI. 202, 203. *Prince Hohenstiel-Schwangau*.
[2] See the Pope's reasons for pronouncing sentence on Guido in *The Ring and the Book* (X), and XV. 47. *Iván Ivánovitch*.
[3] XIII. 350. *Agamemnon*. [4] XV. 57. *Tray*.
[5] IX. 215-239. *Pompilia*. [6] XII. 296.

and tardy softening of a grown-up son and his father. In Browning's Euripides there is a passage on fathers with their lads, in which Herakles naively describes men as 'the children-loving race.'[1] There are Strafford's care for his children, and the advocate's, Don de Archangelis, fussy fondness for his boy of the many diminutives,[2] but, besides these, little or nothing on the subject of child-love in Browning's works. Browning has drawn a whole world of women. One-third of his poetry is on the subject of love, culminating in his personal expression about his wife. The numerous lyrics, scattered about, like jewels, in the hewn gold of his works, are sufficient to redeem him from the charge of constant difficulty and harshness, as, for instance, *The Lost Mistress*, *Round us the wild creatures* in *Ferishtah*, and *Summum Bonum*. Browning's essentially man-like imagination of woman is as subtle and free from commonplace as all his fancy is. He seems peculiarly attracted by an outwardly reserved, inwardly glowing disposition.[3] From *Pauline*, up through *Any Wife to any Husband*, he loves to accentuate woman's best beauty, faithfulness. Men who can die for a principle are not more abundant in Browning than women who can die for a personality. He nobly vindicates women's friendship, women's belief in women, in Guendolen Tresham,[4]

---

[1] XIII. 181.   [2] IX. 242. *The Ring and the Book*.
[3] VI. 125. *My Star*, XIV. 60. *Magical Nature*, XIV. 167. *La Saisiaz* (XIV. 211, 212. *The Two Poets of Croisic* and *Asolando*. 14. *A Pearl, A Girl*.)
[4] IV. 45-51. *A Blot in the 'Scutcheon*.

fighting, like generous Beatrice, against men's cowardice and condemnation. In *Bifurcation*, Browning asserts that mutual love constitutes duty. The woman there called the love-forsaking path duty, but the responsibility of her lover's spoiled life lies at her door. The same idea is still more strikingly brought out in *Cristina*. Browning's handling of love in all its aspects is strong and healthful. To him, earthly marriage is the type and expression of the soul union which consecrates it. An impulse to protect, pity, and console, rather than to worship and take pride in, tinges Browning's vision of love, as in Jules and Phene and the song, "Give her but a least excuse,"[1] and in the 'digression' in *Sordello*.[2] This ministering love, the passion to serve, is also indicated in *The Flight of the Duchess* (V. 146). In simple little Pippa's reverie, love means to be cherished and safely folded with a protector's arm,[3] and in *A Woman's Last Word* a woman's hope of love is the same. But, for all that, Browning maintains that only 'the weaker woman's-want' is to lean, the best women themselves uplift and sustain, so that all their love is a kind of motherhood.[4] In Browning's earliest poem, the *young poet's* belief in love—Pauline's—saves him. Love, purity, devotion, these are the most divine things in the world, and so recognised in his heart of hearts by every character in Browning's works, even by the

[1] III. 44-46. *Pippa Passes*.   [2] I. 159-164. *Sordello*.
[3] III. 11, 12. *Pippa Passes*.
[4] XII. 155. *Red Cotton Night-Cap Country*, and XII. 295, 296. *Inn Album*.

most debased criminal, as in that tremendous last line wrung from Guido Franceschini—

> "Christ,—Maria,—God, . . .
> *Pompilia*, will you let them murder me?"

The poem of the cricket, who supplied the missing string of the lyre, turns on the might of love, as do the Prologue to *Pacchiarotto* and *Wanting is—What?* The eternity of love Browning considers dependent on a mutual response between souls. Love needs soul's beauty to make it live on, the value of bodily beauty is in arousing it.[1] In *Fifine at the Fair*,[2] with seeming ingenuity, but entirely derivatively from his philosophy of individuality, Browning accounts for tastes in faces and forms by saying that the soul sees, consciously or unconsciously, its complement, what it loves, in another soul, a-strain through some bodily token more or less minute, and that it straightway seeks to gain that other soul to amalgamate its own with it. Nature, the imperfect artist, is supplemented, remedied, by the perfect artist, love. But the separate individuality of the soul of each is for ever to be retained and respected. True love and perfect marriage mean union, not unification.[3]

All Browning's dealings with human love are sanctified by his own love for his 'dearest poet,' which over and over again finds expression in his works. Explicitly, he writes of her, during her life, in *By the Fireside*, in *The Guardian-Angel*, incidentally,

---
[1] XII. 273. *Inn Album*.   [2] XI. 254-267.
[3] XII. 92. *Red Cotton Night-Cap Country*.

as '*my* angel,' 'my love,' and in *One Word More, to E. B. B.*; since her death, in *Prospice*, in the 'Invocation,'[1] and end of *The Ring and the Book*, in *Balaustion's Adventure*,[2] where he quotes from her *Wine of Cyprus*, and in the *Epilogue* to *Pacchiarotto*, where he again quotes from the same poem. How many more poems may not be due to the inspiration of his Wife? For in speaking of the explicit reference of *Prospice*, it seems almost arbitrary to exclude '*A Wall*,'[3] and *Wanting is—What?* from the same category. In various touches of description of Browning's favourite women, and in the tender intimacy with a mother's feelings in Pompilia, we may judge how life fed art.

From early youth, Browning was strongly attracted towards Greek life and literature. Perhaps in the very fact that his own mind is pre-eminently Gothic lies the fascination to him of the clear-cut brightness and poignancy of Greece. This interest was strengthened and deepened by Mrs. Browning's classical scholarship. *Balaustion's Adventure* (1871), with the 'Transcript' from Mr. and Mrs. Browning's favourite poet, Euripides, *Aristophanes' Apology* (1875), embodying another transcript, and the *Agamemnon* of Æschylus (1877) sufficiently bear out the presentiment which Browning already had in *By the Fireside* (1855) of how, in the years to come, the study of

---

[1] VIII. 56-57. *The Ring and the Book*.
[2] XI. 121.
[3] (The *Prologue* to *Pacchiarotto with other Poems*.)

Greek would lead him on with increasing force. But it is in independent, short poems and in scattered passages, such as *Artemis Prologizes*, *Pheidippides*, the early lines of *Cleon*, and Prometheus, Artemis, and the nymph and Satyr in *Gerard de Lairesse*, that we get the nearest approach in Browning to Greek presentment.

Another love and source of inspiration to both poet husband and poet wife is Italy, their home for fifteen years. Browning is saturated with the language, art, and history of Italy, and a large proportion of his subjects is Italian. He directly records his love of Italy in *By the Fireside*, "*De Gustibus———*," and the end of *Pietro of Abano*, and he describes Italian natural scenery in *The Englishman in Italy* and many another poem. *Sordello*, *Pippa Passes*, *My Last Duchess*, *In a Gondola*, *The Bishop orders his Tomb at Saint Praxed's Church*, *The Boy and the Angel*, *A Soul's Tragedy*, *Up at a Villa—Down in the City*, *A Toccata of Galuppi's*, *Holy-Cross Day*, *The Guardian-Angel*, *Two in the Campagna*, *The Ring and the Book*, *Pacchiarotto*, *Cenciaja*, *The Cardinal and the Dog*, *The Pope and the Net*, *The Bean Feast*, *Ponte dell' Angelo, Venice*, *Beatrice Signorini*, "*Imperante Augusto natus est———*," are all Italian in characters and circumstances. *Pictor Ignotus*, *Luria*, *Fra Lippo Lippi*, *The Statue and the Bust*, *Andrea del Sarto*, *Old Pictures in Florence*, and *Filippo Baldinucci on the Privilege of Burial* belong especially to Florence. *The Italian in England*, *Old Pictures in Florence*, and "*De Gustibus———*"

express the Italian hate of the foreign rule in Italy, so fervently shared by Robert and Elizabeth Browning. There are other poems, such as *Porphyria's Lover*, *A Face*, *Daniel Bartoli*, and *Francis Furini*, which, even if not definitely placed in Italy, are under Italian influences. The atmosphere of Browning's only drama of English life, *The Blot in the 'Scutcheon*, is Italian rather than English. The criminal, treacherous, magnificent character that fascinated Webster, Tourneur, and Massinger, and all their company has a powerful attraction for the subtle mind of Browning. Of the three or four pages of *The Bishop orders his Tomb at Saint Praxed's Church*, Mr. Ruskin says that the exact temper of the Italian central Renaissance has never been more unerringly discerned. Browning's longest work, however, *The Ring and the Book*, is occupied with a meaner period in Italian annals, the late seventeenth century.

Many of Browning's poems are on Art and artists. His treatment of pictorial art is characteristic, in that he finds his examples in Italy, and that there the early painters, men of lofty aims and imperfect accomplishments, are dearest to him. The advance of the pre-Raphaelites on the Greek sculptors is that while the latter wrought a perfection unattainable by the 'actual generations,' and thereby taught stunted men humility, as well as upheld 'the Truth of Man,' the Italian painters suggested the larger scope by their very defectiveness, and cared most to express the new strife and hopes of the inward and invisible.[1] Browning does not cherish the defects of the early schools as final excellences. In *Fra Lippo Lippi*, he traces the evolution of the next step beyond Giotto and Fra Angelico, art's supreme gift, to make us "love

> First when we see them painted, things we have passed
> Perhaps a hundred times, nor cared to see."

In *Fifine*,[2] Browning deepens this definition by speaking of art as the disinterested, instinctive passion for reaching at all points the truth of things. The artist struggles to make out of nature's scattered fragments a human creation, which shall at once surpass nature and reach reality. Perfectly comprehensible in this connection is Browning's acknowledgment in *Red Cotton Night-Cap Country*[3] that the 'artist-preference' is 'for work complete, inferiorly proposed, to incompletion; though it aim aright.' That preference is an intellectual necessity, because it is part of the work of intellect to rightly adjust means to ends. Meissonier *as an artist* is better than Blake. Only in poetry, which Browning places above art, because nearer the 'soul's verge of vastness,' is the 'incomplete more than completion.' Browning, as an artist, recognises and applauds in artists the perpetual endeavour to obliterate 'Artistry's haunting curse, the Incomplete';[4] as a spectator, he pronounces incompleteness inevitable,

---

[1] VI. 80-86. *Old Pictures in Florence.*
[2] XI. 256.   [3] XII. 168.
[4] X. 210. *The Ring and the Book*, repeated on *Asolando.* 78.

and a blessing, for it goads on to further effort, and points to perfection behind the veil. In *Parleyings*, Browning deals with various art questions. He indignantly opposes the attack on the nude in art, in *Francis Furini*, as he does in *The Lady and the Painter*, and, implicitly, in *Fra Lippo Lippi*, and in *Aristophane's Apology*, XIII. 21, 120. In *Christopher Smart*[1] it is interesting to see what modern painters Browning joins with the august names of Michael Angelo, Rafael, and Leonardo. In the lines in *Aristophanes' Apology*[2] that describe the listeners to Balaustion's adventure, we can fancy Greek girlhood as depicted by Sir Frederick Leighton, who is, in reality, the 'great Kaunian painter'[3] whose work is described in the earlier narrative. In the first section of *Furini*,[4] there is what, if not intended as such, serves as a criticism on the paintings of a great poet, Rossetti. Browning's descriptions of objects of art both steal and give beauty, *e.g.* the della Robbia in *The Statue and the Bust*, the Eastern weapons in *A Forgiveness*, and the font in the castle of Goito.[5] Browning's descriptions constantly suggest pictures. Such are the landscape in "*Childe Roland*," the group of the gipsy queen, the lady, and Jacynth 'in a rosy sleep along the floor,' in *The Flight of the Duchess*, and Pompilia, a portrait with which even Dante's Madonna Pia cannot compare.

[1] XVI. 152.　　　　　　　　[2] XIII. 11.
[3] XI. 121. *Balaustion's Adventure.* (See also *Eurydice to Orpheus*).
[4] XVI. 176, 177.　　　　　　[5] I. 67, 68. *Sordello.*

Browning's love of music has given birth to what is perhaps his most faultless poem, *Abt Vogler*, and to *A Toccata of Galuppi's*, *Master Hugues of Saxe-Gotha*, and *Charles Avison*. Music not only gives Browning intense emotional pleasure, but it is to him the truest truth; how and why are explained in *Avison*.[1]

Browning claims the highest place for poetry, because it 'impinges on and illuminates the other arts.' He throws light on his own poetic methods in the lines

> "Who is a poet needs must understand
> Alike both speech and thoughts which prompt to speak."[2]

Browning draws a sharp line between the dilettant and the artist,[3] and, while giving a grim smile to the former's make-believe, he emphasises the strenuous labour of the artist's life. In *Furini*, he speaks of the 'agony' of 'art's high-strung brain.'[4] In describing poets, Browning constantly dwells on the separateness of the genius and the man, in each. This idea is thoroughly worked out in *Sordello*. Even in *Rabbi Ben Ezra* (xxiii.-xxv.), we meet with a similar view: a man's work is not himself. The same feeling tinges Browning's references to his own poetry. *One Word More* contains a highly poetic expression of this separation between the artist and the man, and

---

[1] XVI. 227, etc.
[2] XII. 138. *Red Cotton Night-Cap Country.*
[3] XII. 89-91. *Red Cotton Night-Cap Country.*
[4] XVI. 179.

Shop sounds, from the other end of the scale, a protest against a man's profession, his 'shop,' constituting his life. There is no doubt that Browning drew the idea from his own experience, and in this way it throws considerable light on the dramatic shape of his mind.

Very beautiful are the wreaths which Browning lays at the feet of his predecessors in the kingdom of poetry. He celebrates Dante in *Sordello* and *One Word More*, and Shelley in *Pauline*, *Sordello*,[1] *Memorabilia*, and *Cenciaja*, as well as in his prose *Introductory Essay to Letters of Percy Bysshe Shelley*, 1852. *Popularity* is sacred to the memory of Keats, who is again referred to in a similar vein at the commencement of *The Two Poets of Croisic*. Beside *At the "Mermaid," House*, and *Aristophanes' Apology*, XIII. 234, Browning has, in *Bishop Blougram's Apology*, at least three vivid lines on Shakspere,

"His power and consciousness and self-delight,"

and

"He leaves his towers and gorgeous palaces
To build the trimmest house in Stratford town."[2]

In *Prince Hohenstiel-Schwangau*,[3] *Fifine*,[4] *Epilogue to Pacchiarotto*,[5] *At the "Mermaid,"*[6] and *La Saisiaz*,[7] Browning derides Byron for his contempt of men and

[1] I. 53-54.
[2] See also V. 248. *Christmas-Eve and Easter-Day*; and Browning's *uncollected* Sonnet, *The Names*.
[3] XI. 145-147.   [4] XI. 277-279.   [5] XIV. 149.
[6] XIV. 35.   [7] XIV. 200-201.

glorification of waste nature, and for his slipshod way of writing; but in *La Saisiaz* a tenderness for the 'Pilgrim' escapes him.[1] Like 'Childe Harold' before him, Browning, in *La Saisiaz*, pauses before those illustrious men of letters who made their homes round Lake Leman. He approaches Voltaire, Gibbon, Rousseau, and Byron himself, to weigh what they gave by what they received. Browning often flashes out a phrase that contains a volume of criticism, as in 'Addison's *tye-wig* preachment,'[2] and it is interesting to note how he esteems a comparatively recent poetical writer, that singular mind, Thomas Lovell Beddoes.[3]

Browning's works almost defy an orderly arrangement according to subjects. Too many a poem eludes classification, or demands a class to itself. Only after reading through the poems in the order in which they were written, do we gain a true idea of Browning's immense range.

5. **The Art of Browning**. — Only those who know Browning intimately can say what an education he is in the resources of language. His memory and circumstantial lore seem boundless. As each of his dissolving views disappears to give place to its successor, Browning seems to steep himself in every appropriate phrase and befitting suggestion that may give vividness to his next creation. We notice instances in *Ned Bratts*, in

[1] XIV. 200, 202-203.   [2] XVI. 120. *Bernard de Mandeville*.
[3] XIV. 270. *The Two Poets of Croisic*.

> "A burden at your back,
> Good Master *Christmas*?"

(Ned Bratts means 'Christian')

> "To-morrow brings Tom Bearward with his bears:
> One new black-muzzled brute beats *Sackerson* he swears."

('Sackerson' was the famous bear kept at Paris Garden), and

> "I rather see the fruit of twelve years' pious reign—
> Astræa Redux, Charles."

Browning might well call himself the 'far-flyer.'[1] He has the curiosities of all dictionaries at his fingers' ends. He uses technical and obsolete words with the most familiar usage, coining new and amplifying old for his purposes. All sorts of colloquialisms and rarities help to feather his dramatic nest. This habit helps to make up the total impression made by Browning of intellectual resource and power. He often repeats his turns of phrase, and many parallelisms may be cited from his works. Such slovenliness as 'better than *them* all' never appears in Browning,[2] his grammar being exquisitely accurate, sometimes even to pedantry. His mental associations are akin to his vocabulary in variety and unexpectedness. As instances, we may take from among his illustrations Goethe's Weimar Estate in *Bernard de Mandeville* and Joan of Arc in *Francis Furini*. Among Browning's finest similes and metaphors are the cabin (sophistical) in *Bishop Blougram's Apology* and

---

[1] XIV. 223. *Charles Avison.*
[2] *e.g.* X. 84. *The Ring and the Book.*

the cup (truthful) in *Rabbi Ben Ezra*. Every allusion is exactly in keeping with the habits of the person who uses it. We note in *An Epistle* how the Arab physician measures the distance between Bethany and Jerusalem,

> "scarce the distance
> A man with plague-sores at the third degree
> Runs till he drops down dead."

Entire freeness from commonplace in imagery and nomenclature distinguishes Browning. With the 'White Way' [1] of *Pauline*, Browning commenced a long series of new names for well-known things, delightful for freshness and the sense of direct impression. Perhaps of all objects in nature he has found the moon most 'noteworthy.'[2] The descriptions of the moon in *Christmas-Eve, One Word More, Pan and Luna*, and the passage from 'Mark the flying orb' to 'one glow and variegation!'[3] in *A Bean-Stripe* are in Browning's finest vein. They have all the charm of eloquence and emotion that can be claimed for poetry. *Parleyings* is rich in day-breaks.[4] The thunder that ushers the day into being, dawning, mid-day, and sunset form the loom on which, in *Gerard de Lairesse*, Browning weaves a web, alternately real and fantastic, though, at the end, the fantastic fails, conquered by the potency of the real. The salute to Spring,[5] in the same poem, is instinct with the modern feeling for nature, which refuses personifications or

[1] I. 19.   [2] IV. 303.   [3] XVI. 72-73.
[4] XVI. 126-127, and 209-216.   [5] XVI. 219-220.

any other derivative sentiments. It delights us by its simple flash of vernal colour and movement, though perhaps, like Shelley's 'West Wind,' it is not far from the kingdom of pathos. Browning gives in *The Inn Album* (XII. 200) a fine bit of English village road, and the woods under the sunset[1] in *Sordello* form another of Browning's beauties of description. We have, too, in Introduction and Part I. of *Pippa Passes* wonderful representations of the glare of Italian morning, and in *La Saisiaz* as faithful glimpses of the mountain sides round the Lake of Geneva. Browning's observation is pre-eminently original. He notices, treasures, and uses what others might meet with and pass again and again, as in his comment on the myth of Hercules and Atlas.[2] This is Browning's value to us, he so enriches observation, reflection, and love. In reading his works, we experience the exhilaration that comes from contact with a forceful personality. He catches us up in the free play of his genius over the whole visible and invisible world, every thing of both lying before him, he only having to choose what shall serve him on each occasion. If we wrestle, it is with an angel. If the reading be strenuous, it imparts life, and a strange power seems to pass from him to us. For the time being, we see ourselves as coloured by a stripe of his rainbow genius.

Less often *possessed* by his theme, and therefore less passionately imaginative than Shakspere or Coleridge, Browning not infrequently reaches their

[1] I. 54.   [2] XI. 153.

white-heat of intensity. One example of this is in Caponsacchi's Dantesque forecast of Guido, left by his judges to 'live,' and how, when he dies, or at least disappears from among men, he will find only Judas to be his companion, 'the cockatrice' met 'with the basilisk.'[1] Browning's works abound in grotesqueness and humour. That Browning is intensely capable of the ludicrous is clear from such a passage as that in which the advocate deplores for Caponsacchi the companionship on the drive to Rome of

> "only one young female substitute
> For seventeen other Canons of ripe age
> Were wont to keep him company."[2]

Sometimes we find the humour of a single word, as in one physician writing to another,

> "Scalp-disease
> Confounds me, crossing so with leprosy:
> Thou hadst *admired* one sort I gained at Zoar."[3]

Browning is a wonderful and versatile rhymer. Nothing daunts him. Sustained double rhymes, as in *A Grammarian's Funeral*, are his daily wear. *Through the Metidja* is a triumph of rhymes on one word only. Browning revels in whimsicalities, as in *The Flight of the Duchess* and *The Pied Piper*. *Pacchiarotto* is a carnival of rhymes. They pour out as in some uproarious game of capping rhymes and rapping rhymes. *Pietro of Abano* shows Browning's

---

[1] IX. 159-160. *The Ring and the Book.*
[2] X. 28. *The Ring and the Book.*
[3] IV. 188. *An Epistle.*

metrical ability, and *Ixion* is a skilful example of hexameters and pentameters. With extreme effectiveness, the beat of the verse in *Ivàn Ivànovitch* is changed after the first distant 'pad' of the wolves, so that the woman's tight breathing, and the terrible excitement of that most nightmare-like fear of being gained upon by the four-footed demons seem to inspire its hard pulses, through which we hear too the ever nearing 'pad,' 'pad,' and at last the horrid onset. *The Last Ride Together* may be counted among Browning's most musical productions.

6. **Browning as a Writer of Plays.**—Humanity is the theme of drama, action its instrument. A drama is an organic structure of interesting events which are the interaction of its characters. No dramatist ever took a keener interest in human beings than Browning, nor felt more strongly that they must be represented dramatically to be represented truthfully, must not be described as from without, but must speak for themselves as from within. Accordingly, Browning's vivid, picturesque poems abound in one great dramatic quality, characterisation. *My Last Duchess, A Light Woman, A Forgiveness* prove Browning's mastery of dramatic material. To this he adds forcible objective realisation of the great moments of life. If his poems display material for dramatic situations, his plays are rich in situations themselves, as in the night of Luria's death, the alternations of false and true kingliness in Victor and Charles, and that great

scene in which Strafford drains the cup of anguish.[1] For tragic terror it would be hard to match the dialogue between Ottima and Sebald in *Pippa Passes*. Yet, when all is said, Browning's plays are not dramas, but studies. They are without the light and shade, the inevitable cohesion and the indubitable conclusion that are the distinguishing marks of a great drama. Their beauties are inorganic or fragmentary. A complex but indissoluble action is the very life of drama, whereas Browning cares little for action and sacrifices it to soliloquy. His eight plays represent the dynamics of the soul rather than of incident. He is more occupied with the intricacies of motive than with its fruit in conduct. Probably Browning's century does not excel in the kind of greatness that stimulates drama. Its subjective character, its introspection, its self-absorption are all opposed to the objective character of dramatic genius. In Browning's eyes, the more internal, the more real, but the invisible, however momentous, is apt to be ineffectual in drama, and, if not that, its expression comes too near showing machinery that should be hidden. Neither should a play, which is primarily intended for acting, strain the mental attention as severely as a poem intended for reading may do. The piece hastens on, and no halt, no retracing are possible. Browning expects of his audience transitions of mind as swift and subtle as his own. Too much is taken as said, and the

[1] II. 290-307. *Strafford*.

speeches, besides being frequently of immoderate length, are difficult from extreme condensation. As a playwright, Browning lacked acquaintance with theatrical conditions and verisimilitudes,[1] which even such a born dramatist as Shakspere could ill have spared. It may be said of Browning that, adjectively dramatic, he is not substantively a dramatist. Urged, at first, to drama by the qualities in him which were dramatic, with time he wisely forsook the limitations of the theatre, and created for himself a fitter instrument in the dramatic monologue, the form of so many of his greatest poems. Mental debates in character, both debates and characters being extremely interesting in themselves, they are properly independent of stage and footlights.

7. Defects and Difficulties.—Browning has not an infallible metrical ear. His metres are frequently unsuited to his themes. *Christmas-Eve* contains doggerel rhymes that give to their great argument an alien air of burlesque, as if a seer broke off in the midst of his vision to turn wheels like a street arab. *Sordello* would have been ennobled and liberated by blank verse. The *Prologue* to *Parleyings* has a falsely archaic air from being a conversation arranged in stanzas, recalling some old Mystery or Miracle Play. It is an altogether anomalous metrical arrangement. In these examples, and wherever his rhymes and fancies pour out in pell-mell confusion, Browning shows a want of the selectiveness of fine art. 'Mind-

---

[1] See Song in *A Blot in the 'Scutcheon.*

Freaks'[1] is an expression used by Browning which fits many passages in his own writings, where the liberty of power degenerates into licence. After the poetical line in *Popularity*,

"The sea has only just o'erwhispered!"[2]

one shrinks from

"As if they still the *water's lisp heard*"

as from an unexpected, intentional rudeness. Browning's rhymes often coerce his ideas, leading him off after them into some parenthesis or congested allusion from which he re-emerges, with great cleverness, no doubt, but with cleverness that seems a blot on genius. If in some places Browning makes mere rhyme the pivot of the sense, in others he neglects rhythm. His blank verse is sometimes regardless of scansion, and not true blank verse at all. His poetry is often unpoetic by reason of its crabbedness and harshness, its lack of grace and melody, as in

"Irks care the crop-full bird? Frets doubt the maw-crammed beast?"[3]

Browning perpetually makes polysyllabic superlatives, for compression's sake, as 'portentousest,'[4] 'sagaciousest.'[5] A crudity disfigures the close of *Furini* in

"Memorize that *burst's moment*, Francis!"[6]

---

[1] XV. 94. *Clive.*   [2] VI. 194.
[3] VII. 110. *Rabbi Ben Ezra.*
[4] VIII. 9. *The Ring and the Book.*
[5] XV. 49. *Iván Ivánovitch.*   [6] XVI. 199.

A string of 'possessives' is not rare, as

"The strong fierce *heart's love's labour's* due."[1]

Browning's works are professedly not meant for a slothful or inattentive reader. Browning's intellectual processes are performed so rapidly, his turns of thought are so abrupt, that a less leaping, less impetuous brain is apt to consider the expression of such velocity incoherent. Stringent reasoning, of which there is so much in Browning, is necessarily hard to follow, and demands considerable stress of attention. But most of his verbal difficulties proceed from condensation. Sordello's sources of feeling are no more remote than Hamlet's, but the expression of them is infinitely more crumpled. As a specimen of close packing, see

" Etrurian circlets found . . .
. . . alive
Spark-like 'mid unearthed slope-side figtree-roots,
That roof old tombs at Chiusi."[2]

At first, the reader's comprehension seems often to be balancing on a tight-rope, where the slightest touch would be dangerous, and, if it comes, in the shape of an additional difficulty, does indeed precipitate the already faltering comprehension into an abyss of bewilderment. Comparative ease in reading Browning being due to familiarity with his peculiarities, the following notes may prove useful finger-

[1] XV. 196. *Mary Wollstonecraft and Fuseli.*
[2] VIII. 1. *The Ring and the Book.*

posts. There is in Browning's sentences a frequent omission . . . of relatives, *e.g.*

"Hold her tottering ark [*that* or *which*] had tumbled else"[1]

. . . of 'pronominal' adjectives, *e.g.*

"Doff [your] spectacles, wipe [your] pen, shut [your] book"[2]

. . . of *to* with the infinitive, *e.g.*

"Mend matters peradventure God loves [to] mar?"[3]

Readers have to become used to a general scarcity of prepositions, as well as of conjunctions, *e.g.*

"The gap 'twixt what is, [and] what should be."[4]

Pronouns sometimes precede by several lines the nouns for which they stand. Dialogues within dialogues are another source of difficulty. Readers have often to look several lines forward to help their notion of the sense by finding whether the expected note of interrogation ends the sentence. Notes of interrogation are very frequent, especially in the poems of internal debate, or where casuistry meets casuistry. Inversions are characteristic, *e.g.*

"Of joy were it fuller, of span because ampler?"[5]

Any dozen pages of Browning contain a volume's references to history and biography, and question and research are being continually aroused. Brown-

---

[1] VIII. 9. *The Ring and the Book.*
[2] XI. 207. *Prince Hohenstiel-Schwangau.*
[3] VIII. 221. *The Ring and the Book.*
[4] IX. 102. *The Ring and the Book.*
[5] XVI. 101. *Apollo and the Fates.*

ing loves to go off at a tangent. He follows up a branch line with as much interest as though it were his main theme. He is a 'creeper into wormholes,' and the obscurities and unknowns of the past are more to him than its great events and trampling conquerors. Yet Browning's hardest lines are no harder to subject to grammatical analysis than many in *Paradise Lost.* The worst that can be said of his roughness and difficulty is as much as to say : here is pure gold, but it is uncoined and must be dug for, and certain fragments of rock are sticking to the nuggets.

There is another valid charge brought against Browning, a charge which the reputation of many a leading poet has encountered and survived, that of inequality of poetic inspiration. Large portions of Browning's works are, from the poetic stand-point, comparatively sterile. Good sense and pungency are rarely, if ever, lacking to a single line, but these are the virtues of the prosaist, not the wonder-work of emotion and word without which great poetry is not. Much of *La Saisiaz* is too polemical for poetry. Those 'five facts' and 'six facts' (XIV. 193, 194), are not poetry, but 'divinity.' The Pope's meditation in *The Ring and the Book* is poetically finer, partly because the theology is subordinated to the character of the Pope, and consequently the presentment is more imaginative. Mere serpentinings of thought and hair-splittings cannot of themselves reach that incandescent point at which poetry is struck from the anvil. Prince Hohenstiel - Schwangau's special pleading is metrical prose, with most occasional gleams of poetry. Browning's later characters are too eager to 'try conclusions' with their outside adversary or inner tempter, too intent to 'read their title clear' to theism and immortality, in a word, too argumentative for poetic creations. Though Browning reached his high-water mark in the vital monologues of *The Ring and the Book*, his short poems, such as are to be found in the volumes of Selections, contain his most flawless poetry. To cover his work, and not only account for special portions of it, it must e'en be conceded that truth is more to Browning than beauty. What is this but saying that the man is greater than the artist? Truly, a brave sin, and one which more than ever confirms the sense of unity in Browning's personality and all its output. Browning's poetics manifest a temporary decline in *Prince Hohenstiel-Schwangau*, *Fifine at the Fair*, and *Aristophanes' Apology*. These books are thorny reading, and in them, and more especially in *Red Cotton Night-Cap Country*, Browning's passion for strange backwaters of character takes him among that which is morally ugly and even worthless. Browning's optimism is a stumbling-block to some readers, and certainly it does not leave him much room for ultimate pathos. Whether, in this, Browning does well or ill depends on whether his root belief, that no failure is final, be well founded or no. The question is wider than a criticism of Browning.

CHAPTER III.

INTRODUCTIONS TO THE POEMS.

Pauline ; A Fragment of a Confession, 1833 (Vol. I.), was the first work Browning gave the world. In conformity with an intention of youth, he issued it anonymously. The word 'Richmond,' added to the date at the end, was a fiction, intended to baffle readers. *Pauline* was not included among Browning's works till the edition of 1868, when, for necessary reasons, 'with extreme repugnance' he acknowledged and retained it. He made some slight corrections for the 1888 edition. *Pauline*, by an unknown poet, met with little general notice. Two great men, separate enough, Stuart Mill and Dante Rossetti, were much struck by it, Rossetti divining that the writer of *Pauline* was the Browning of *Paracelsus*. The motto from the old French of Clément Marot, "I am no longer—I could never be again—what I was," is the burden of the 'Confession.' The preface of Cornelius Agrippa suggests that Browning cared to 'half reveal and half conceal' a partial identity between his own youthful mind and the mind of the young poet who is supposed to be speaking—or writing—throughout. 'Pauline' herself only speaks once, as supposed editress of the fragment, in a prose note in French. She is represented by *the poet* as a wise, calm friend, unfailing in her devotion to him, forgiving the inconstancy and degradation he has previously confessed to her, for a former confession is referred to (pp. 5, 6), the result of which emboldens this one. If we were to take dramatically Pauline's note, in which she speaks of her 'pauvre ami' in a tone of pitying patronage, her calm would be more apparent than her love, but the note, with its very just criticism, is in fact Browning's, not 'Pauline's.' As a foretaste of the sanity and reflectiveness of Browning's genius, it is extremely interesting. It shows the youth of twenty, looking at his just written poem, and even then recognising its indistinctness, fitfulness, and lack of balance. Throughout the Confession, the young *poet's* vivid imagination of Pauline makes him address her as if she, with her 'soft breast' and 'sweet eyes,' were listening to his words, though he is really alone, writing what she is to read (see Pauline's note, p. 36). The chief things *the poet* has to confess are the faults of a genius ahead of moral judgment. He records no incidents, only the phases of thought and feeling which underlay action, or were in great part their own end, for he exaggerates his faults, and is abnormally sensitive about merely imaginative sins —perhaps, after all, as 'real' to this typical idealist as matter-of-fact offences. Excess of imagination combined with moral wavering (p. 42), self-absorption, restless craving after unattainable joy and beauty, have driven his now exhausted mind into every untenable extreme. He bitterly regrets his loss of the freshness of youth (p. 8), his powers of concentration foregone (pp. 27, 28), his aimless, truthless, unloving state. He sadly tells Pauline how, lured by beauty in strange eyes, he has broken his allegiance. Much of his experience resembles that of Paracelsus and Sordello. He is a sketch for their finished portraits. Like Paracelsus, he craves for knowledge (p. 28), and for a time makes that his god. Still more like Aprile, and with the same artistic and poetic temperament, he forsakes duty to follow after loveliness. Most like Sordello, in his 'first dawn of life' he fancies himself all the bright heroes of childhood (p. 16), and, grown man, resembles him in despair of translating his passion and insight into any form that can influence the many (pp. 19-25), and so essays to be himself his All-in-all (p. 31). Like those other three, the mind of this first of Browning's characters clears again (pp. 39, 40, 45). Through all his wanderings, he never loses sight of some fixed stars. His 'yearning after God' (pp. 15, 37), partly obscured by a fatuous fatalism (p. 15), never dies, and he longs to see and be loved by Christ (p. 38). Then, too, introductory to the beautiful address in which Browning glorifies Shelley under the title of 'Sun-treader' (pp. 9, 10, 11), *the poet* says—

> "the glow I felt at HIS (*i.e.* Shelley's) award
> Assured me all was not extinct within."

He speaks of first poetic efforts being half original, half imitative (p. 19), and the reader hears echoes of Shelley in various lines. The poem closes with an invocation to him. At that time Browning was steeped in Shelley. He has always expressed intense admiration for the earlier poet, the most aerial charming the most indubitably human! Music is another voice that appealed to Pauline's lover. In this first work, Browning speaks of music (p. 18) as the one language of innermost soul, not mind, exactly as in *Abt Vogler* (1864) and *Charles Avison* (1887). One speaks advisedly of Browning's continuous unity of thought and purpose! Again, *the poet* speaks of the limitless dreams opened to him by Plato (p. 20), but at the failure (p. 21) of such hopes of life's perfectibility he denies all goodness (p. 22). This dark mood is too foreign to his nature to last. Beauty and desire are stronger temptations than negation to this poet as typical as Keats. Browning's intense susceptibility to the charm of Greek life and myth are as marked in *Pauline* as ever later. Whenever, even in his most analytic years, Browning approaches Hellas, he becomes simpler and more direct, his hand to a perceptible extent subdued to what it works in. That cameo, the passage that describes Andromeda (pp. 29, 30), would grace the finest anthology. The lines referring to Agamemnon, Ajax, and Orestes (p. 26), and the 'pale sister,' Antigone (p. 43) are equally poetical. Separated in subject, yet akin in interpenetrative imagination, are the lines on Christ's sorrow and triumph (p. 38). England was a potent word to Browning (pp. 31, 43) while Italy was still unknown earth. *The poet* and Pauline are to go to her native pines and snows, there his humility and her love shall fit him for truer life. *Pauline* is fuller of 'poets' poetry' and of nature than any later work. The faithful reporting of nature, after impassioned contemplation of it, in such passages as the spring morning (p. 5), the bird mounting the tree (p. 32), the pool (p. 33), the forest water (p. 34), those Shelleyan snakes, and, not least, the living nature of Pauline's eyes and cheeks and neck (p. 40) need no commentator. Though full of poetry in 1832, Browning had not yet found his true walk, *i.e.* souls dramatically revealed, poetry resting on a substantial prose basis.

Paracelsus, 1835 (Vol. II.), met, on publication, with at all events one competent reviewer. In his article, 'Evidences of a New Dramatic Poetry,' John Forster wrote, "Mr. Browning is a man of genius, he has in himself all the elements of a great poet, philosophical as well as dramatic." *Paracelsus* is chiefly in dialogue, but though in one sense intensely dramatic, the poem is no drama, and, by a note to the first edition, Browning secured it from being so regarded. Incidents take no part in *Paracelsus*, though it is less remote from action than *Pauline*, and, to a much greater extent, its crises of thought and feeling presage or follow events. The narrative is definite, 'no problem for the fancy but a life spent and decided' (pp. 40, 41). Browning's erudite, eight-paged note at the end of the poem gives history's account of Bombastus Paracelsus (1493-1541), a famous name in the progress of chemistry and medical science, a 'prodigious genius,' according to Lavater. He was German or German-Swiss, contemporary with Luther, Zuinglius, Erasmus, and Frobenius. He introduced the use of mercury and laudanum, and his writings foreshadow some of the most productive discoveries of modern times. Wonderful tales were told of magic residing in his sword, Azoth. The discoverer of laudanum was naturally associated with sorcery, at a date when the Ages of Roger Bacon, elixir vitæ, and the philosopher's stone had scarcely succumbed to printing and Luther. Paracelsus himself sought science through astrology and alchemy, and, if research and experiment scattered his belief, he continued to impose on others' credulity. As a lecturer he was boastful and domineering, and instead of answering the sages, burned their books. Exposed as an impostor, he had to vacate his Basel professorship. He wandered through many lands, restlessly pursuing knowledge. The father of chemistry, a world benefactor, a drunkard and pretender, he died in a hospital cell. This was history's Paracelsus. What is Browning's? *Paracelsus* is in five parts; in the first, Paracelsus is on the eve, perhaps in the midst, of a crisis. The last links between the lowly charities of home feelings and his proud, unquestioning flight are snapping in this Würzburg garden, where 'Paracèlsus aspires' to knowledge. Part I. is a conversation between him and Festus, with an occasional word from sweet Michal. This night precedes the departure of Paracelsus on his quest. Festus, who has always adored his genius, prophesied his transcendency, and cherished his spirit (p. 11), now, when Paracelsus touches 'the brink of his design' (p. 11), seems faint-heartedly dissuading him from what his previous encouragements might have prepared him for. He is really dissuading him from the immolation of all life's good except what comes from grappling physics and metaphysics to force them to render up the wonderful secret which Paracelsus believes can, when once seized, be wrung out in one ineffable moment to raise and magnify mankind. Paracelsus abjures Black Arts (p. 19), "too intimate a tie connects him with God," but in his undisciplined expectation of some universal secret he belongs to a half art, half science period. Paracelsus starts with entire self-confidence (p. 20), and a convenient belief that he is God's organ (pp. 17, 27-28), working God's will. In sublime prophecy, pathetic in the light of subsequent non-fulfilment, he declares his conviction of 'God's commission' to him (p. 11) to go forth and conquer knowledge for mankind. There is already a vague sophisticalness, a mixture of motives, in Paracelsus. We share the sadness and doubts of Festus whose hero-worship of his friend and agreement with his theories are disturbed by an uneasy instinct he is powerless to define that 'Aureole' is entering on a self-willed, arrogant course. At every objection Festus raises, Paracelsus routs his arguments, floods him with oratorical rhetoric (p 20), or stuns him with his self-belief. He further confounds his impressible, somewhat ineffectual friend by a genuine sympathy with his ideals, a true sense of what he himself renounces. Paracelsus, Festus presently acknowledges, is so exceptional that he does right to take an exceptional course. God has a special message to deliver by such angel-men, and woe to the dullards who would restrain them. Paracelsus mistakenly imagines his 'vast longings' God-sent (p. 13), and, ignorant of himself, condemns those who believe in their 'innate strength' (p. 17). Festus timidly questions the sincerity of his friend's self-annihilation in devotion to 'God's will,' whether, for all he fancies, a more personal ambition does not mingle with the nobler one, whether he discerns his path clear as his desire (pp. 17-18). With overwhelming eloquence, Paracelsus deprecates rather than meets this objection (p. 19). Then Festus urges the solidarity of great thinkers. Should not Paracelsus rather receive learning's torch from Aristotle (p. 22), and pass it on, than stand solitary? If Paracelsus really cared for truth, he would gladly accept it from whatever source (p. 22). Paracelsus reveals his weakness in his contempt of men (p. 24), his standing, even while their benefactor, aloof from their lives (pp. 29, 30). He fancies it disinterestedness, and the voice which whispers so, God's voice (p. 26). Of course there is also the nobly scientific spirit in his determination to take nothing on trust, to lightly esteem knowledge at second-hand, and insist on interrogating nature direct. In reading pp. 26, 27, we yearn towards Paracelsus, who is most self-sacrificing as we commonly count sacrifice, and whose faults are "brave sins which saint when shriven." Paracelsus points to the sages' failure in remedying misery (p. 28); he will adventure apart from their lore. Michal's readier womanly belief entirely elicited (pp. 28, 29, 38), she yet joins Festus in predicting danger from spurning love and fellow-feeling (pp. 30, 31). Paracelsus asserts that absolute knowledge is shut in a man's breast, to be extracted thence (pp. 34, 35), not, as he finds later (p. 169), to penetrate therein by experience and painful toils. Paracelsus entertains hopes, significant, in their unjustifiableness, of his almost unconscious defect (p. 37). His outlook is terribly far from the perfect outlook described in *Sordello*, the two sights God has conceded man. Paracelsus has the sight of the 'whole work,' he ignores, or confounds with it, the 'minute's work.'

By Part II., nine years have elapsed, and Paracelsus is at Constantinople, at a fortune-teller's he has stooped to consult. He has just written, in the guest-book, the sum of his life thus far, and he makes this a halting-point whence to review his gains. We know they are disappointing before he counts them.

Wasted in strength, lowered in spirit (p. 48), inserting his chronicle among others still more unsound (p. 40), he is despising the dupes around him equally with the Greek adept. His hunger for knowledge has become wolfish (p. 44), he can no longer control it (p. 45). On pp. 47, 48, 49 he reaches a climax of bitterness, after which he reflects that, after all, since God has not sent a warning like Constantine's cross (p. 50), he must yet be meant for great things. Here Aprile's wail breaks in. The Italian poet, the 'lover, had tried to live by art, beauty, and emotion, as the German philosopher, the 'knower,' by science, power, and intellect. Both fail because each is half of a dissevered whole (p. 65). The Shelley-like Aprile gives glorious expositions of the artist's passion (pp. 56-64). Though his trials have been different, Paracelsus is pierced when Aprile attributes his own failure to having gazed upon the prize till blinded to the 'patient toil' (p. 59). Finally they bind themselves, Paracelsus, to love; Aprile, to know; but the tenderness of Parcelsus cannot save Aprile's life. He dies, leaving Paracelsus with one first attainment—the discovery that love must work with knowledge.

In Part III., Paracelsus is a lecturer at Basel. Apparently he has learned little from Aprile. That germ has yet to develop. To illustrate to Festus his interest in simple life, Paracelsus describes (p. 72) a death-bed he has lately tended. This passage is worthy to be placed beside Shakspere's death of Falstaff. Paracelsus explains his half mocking, half wistful talk by confessing his deterioration. He is dissatisfied with his discoveries (pp. 90, 91), and disgusted at the stupid opposition of his patients and of his disciples (pp. 84-87, 92)—to whom he gives only inferior knowledge (p. 104). Former hopes gone, he is enslaved by former habits of thought. He has reached the obverse of his infatuated idea of God's will (p. 88), confesses his sensual excesses, and admits his failure in assimilating Aprile's lesson (pp. 95, 96). Festus tries to calm his maddened talk (p. 101). Again the only solution for Festus is in believing his friend beyond men's scope of judgment (p. 102). Lastly, Paracelsus sadly acknowledges that 'love, hope, fear, faith,' and not intellectual gains disparted from these, 'make humanity.' He is learning, but slowly as yet.

Part IV. shows Paracelsus in the depths of outward degradation. Liechtenfels, referred to here, was a patient, recovered by laudanum, who refused his fee. The authorities being applied to, Paracelsus raised such a brawl against them, that he had to leave Basel for Alsatia. Again 'aspiring,' but in a reckless, revengeful mood, he explains to Festus that he re-embraces his earliest aims (p. 118), but sings, in an exquisite lyric, the requiem of the old means (p. 119). He now intends to enjoy and know (p. 121). Presently he subsides into feverish self-loathing (pp. 124, 137), calling his life only a makeshift, a shuffling to the grave. By a parable, itself a splendid poem, complete, musical, and clear, he symbolises the fate of mistaken choosers who "have no heart" to choose afresh. Festus (p. 134) blames Paracelsus for his want of humility, his attempted tyranny over God. Only in that way, Paracelsus replies, can such as he serve God (p. 135). Again, Festus shrinks from condemnation. An exquisite gleam occurs when Paracelsus, with unusual humility, expresses his hope of immortality. The solemn newness of his belief is unmeaning to the tame orthodoxy of Festus.

In Part V. we come to the last Attainment. The tender friend seeks to pierce the dying man's lethargy. Thoughts of Aprile (p. 145), the torture men's scorn has cost him (p. 153), a recollected visit to a witch (p. 148), swim before Paracelsus. Festus, like Browning's David, recites a sweet nature-poem (p. 158) and soon after a great quietness falls on Paracelsus. In his person, Browning expresses a doctrine, frequent in his works, rather to be felt than defined, *i.e.* that God's praise rises in any case, and that He sees deeper in forming his praisers and their way of praising than men guess (pp. 164, 165). Paracelsus has a magnificent vision of creation, culminating in its interpreter, man. Each phase of earth's evolution is a thrill of God's joy. Man has to love, learn, be patient. But evolution has not ended with humanity as we know it; the race is to be liberated and perfected in each of its members, and to help this forward men like Paracelsus are born. Patience, sympathy, wisdom were what he lacked. He now comprehends all, and hopefully his great soul disappears.

Strafford; A Tragedy, 1837 (Vol. II.), came out a year after the Life of Strafford in Lardner's *Eminent British Statesmen.* This life, published under Forster's name, was completed, perhaps chiefly written by Browning with materials supplied by Forster, who was ill and anxious about the volume's completion. Whatever may have been the extent of Browning's assistance to Forster, the biography furnished the basis and point of view[1] of the drama, and is an invaluable companion to it.

Act I., Scene 1. The play opens in November (or September), 1639. Ireland is under sword-law and the Scots' Parliament is just dissolved. England has had no Parliament for ten years, and her leaders believe that the growing despotism is due to the 'apostate,' Wentworth. The fervent Vane, the moderate Hampden, Rudyard, even Wentworth's brother-in-law, Hollis, are gathering up their pent indignation to bring him to doom. Only Pym believes that, from very disgust with Charles, his once dear friend may yet be theirs. In Scene 2, Lady Carlisle, who loves the stern, heroic Wentworth, reveals to him the Queen and Court's ill-will. Wentworth, wholly absorbed in king-worship, but worn and broken by the half trust reposed in him by Charles, has been meanly summoned to undertake the Scots' war, to thrust Laud's Service-book down their throats at the sword's point. He entirely deprecates the

[1] See Preface to first edition of *Strafford*.

expedition, though he is to bear its odium. With noble, disarming honesty, Pym strives to regain him, but no deviation of career is possible to Wentworth. Created Earl, Strafford begs his kingly idol to summon Parliaments, both for levies, and support against Scotland. The taunts of the pernicious Queen soon obliterate in Charles the uncongenial influence for constitutional instrumentation. In Act II., the Short Parliament has been convened, to be outraged by a demand for twelve subsidies (about £840,000). The leaders' bitterness waxes. Only Pym's hope of Strafford is augmented by Charles's speedy dissolution of Parliament. In Scene 2, Strafford finds himself shamefully crossed by Charles in his plans for the 'Bishops' war.' He almost reviles the unthankful King, whose one care is to screen himself behind Strafford's thorough devotion, but, Pym and Hampden entering, stronger instincts rush back, and Strafford, solemnly challenged by the disillusioned Pym to answer for his crimes, tenderly warned by Lady Carlisle, the storm gathering darkly around him, hurries from the presence to fulfil the King's will. By Act III., Scene 1, the Long Parliament has been reluctantly called (November 3rd, 1640). Foiled by the Scots, Charles, without consulting Strafford, has made a truce. This is England's turning-point. The Commons, not the King, are now supreme, and their first work is to arraign Strafford. In this juncture (Scene 2), Charles has selfishly summoned him to help him through a critical time, though all know that Strafford sacrifices every chance of safety by appearing in London. When, with unswerving fidelity, he arrives, a new energy inspires him. He reveals to Lucy Percy his intention of impeaching Pym and the 'Cabal' for treasonably inviting a Scots invasion. She cannot bear to tell him that his own impeachment is in hand. Scene 3 depicts the hub-bub near the doors of the House while Pym's attack on Strafford is going on. On learning his fall, Strafford again almost abjures his false master. In Act IV., Scene 1, we are in the midst of Strafford's Trial. Hollis is at Whitehall to find whether the King will be heartless enough to escape by throwing Strafford to the people. After much wretched shuffling, Charles engages in a desperate plan—depending, however, on Strafford's unlikely assent—to save him by the army. Meanwhile Strafford has defended himself with colossal ability, basing his replies on the novel meaning his opponents put to 'treason.' (Scene 2) It is in vain. Pym concentrates every engine, bars every escape. Vane, Rudyard, Fiennes beseech him to stop short of the Bill of Attainder, but the public security is Pym's supreme law, and England requires Strafford's death. In Scene 3, Pym, disregarding Charles's promises and penitence, warns him of the danger of refusing his assent to the death-warrant, and thereby wrings the act of infamy from him. Act V. opens with Lady Carlisle's scheme of rescuing Strafford. Scene 2 represents Strafford imprisoned, still trusting to the

King's plighted word to save him. Hollis shatters this remnant of faith, to leave Charles writhing in ineffectual remorse before his martyr. The plan of rescue, accepted by Strafford for his master's sake, is averted by Pym. At last, the two men stand face to face as men, and no longer as embodied forces, despotism incarnated in Strafford, despotism's vengeance in Pym. In the new light of ruin and death, Wentworth partly descries that his love for England has worn the mask of hate, and that Pym, not himself, has been her real helper. But still the ruling passion is devotion to the Stuart, 'the man and not the king,'[1] whose life Strafford, foreseeing the future, implores Pym to spare.

Truth to character rather than historical precision of facts and events is the aim of the drama. It is in this play following on *Paracelsus*, that Browning's strong sympathy with the world's failures begins to impress us. Unlike Charles I., Browning *is*

"of those who care the more for men
That they're unfortunate."[2]

Sordello, 1840 (Vol. I.), is the story of a poet's inner life. Difficulties of composition are greater in *Sordello* than in any other of Browning's works. Tantalising and tedious in parts, it is to many readers his most fascinating poem, over which his unique imagination seems to brood most lovingly. The prefatory letter is *Sordello's* most valuable comment.

[1] p. 241.   [2] p. 237.

The continuous headings, added in 1863 and designed to explain the poem, are absent from the last edition. Browning seems to tell Sordello's [1] story just as it first struck and shaped itself to him, an inartistic, though natural, process. Tiraboschi, *Storia della Letteratura Italiana*, IV. 360, and Muratori, *Annali d'Italia, Tomo Settimo*, may be referred to, the one for suppositions concerning Sordello's identity and career, the other for the historical characters and facts the form and pressure of which compose the background. The skeleton of the poem is as follows. Book the First. Place, Verona; period, early thirteenth century. Pp. 52-54—To hear his unexampled story, Browning summons dead and living. He gives two scenes of a night in Verona. (1) In the market-place. 55—Disturbing news has come that the city's prince, Richard of Saint Boniface, ally of Azzo of Este, the Guelf 'lion,' is entrapped in Ferrara, while seeking to thrust thence Taurello Salinguerra, Ecelin Romano's supporter. (67—Struggles preceding Richard's capture are narrated.) 56-63 — Envoys, burghers, fighters help Browning to describe the embroilment. The Lombard League, fifteen cities, must ransom Richard. The Emperor's descent on Italy is feared. 59, 60—His barons are compared to sea rocks, the more democratic Papal party to the growth of weed. 61—The naturalisation of the formidable family of Ecelo ('hill-cat') is described. (2) Inside Richard's palace. 63, 64—The heroine has just left Sordello, at some crisis, but for us a glimpse only.

---

[1] See Dante, *Purgatorio*, VI. 58-81.

65 — Browning turns and proposes to disentwine Sordello, Dante's forerunner in Italian literature, from the great name in which his own has become lost. 66 — We are moved back thirty years, and within Goito Castle, in Mantuan land, a lonely boy feeds his imagination from carvings and tapestry. This castle is Ghibellin Adelaide the Tuscan's, Ecelin's wife. 69—Here too lives Palma (Dante's 'Cunizza'), Ecelin's daughter by Agnes of Este. Sordello's poetical temperament is described in a look forward, not this time into his 'out-world,' but into his developing character. 72—He is of the better class of poets, separate from, and above their works. 73—Two dangers threaten such, inactivity through despair of achievement, and impotent strife for completeness. Both forms of 'leprosy' will be Sordello's. 75— The mystery and isolation of the child's life are traced. 78—Naddo, the Trouvere, is common-place sense incarnated. 76, 77—Sordello outgrows contentment with the 'pretend' life of unresponding flowers. 80—He yearns to surpass and impress a world more real than the woodland. 82—His simulacrum of men is unsatisfactory, but he will make it suffice. 83—The boy cannot equal his heroes, 84— except in fancy, which, therefore, for the present, he deifies, 85—and imagines himself ideal strength and grace combined, 86—Apollo. 88—Apollo demands Daphne. Palma (designed as bride for Richard—to ally Este) is she.

Book the Second. 29—Dreaming of Palma, Sor-

dello comes upon her at a poetical tournament. 94
—Eglamor's (Richard's Troubadour) 'Elys' theme
is excelled in by Sordello, who, 95—amid applause,
is made Palma's minstrel. 96, 97—Dazed till alone,
Sordello ponders the supremacy of song. 98—Eglamor, dead of defeat, is carried past. 99—To such
as Eglamor, art is the god they serve. 102—Sordello
pays tribute to the corpse, whence a symbol flower
springs. 103—Sordello must learn his origin. 104
—Alas, he is a common archer's child, but, 105—
knowing his mental rarity, he means yet to master the
world by his will, 106—for he can enter into all
ideals, 107—is no mere slave of one. 107—What
self-importance to be quenched! 108 — Sordello
expects by consciousness of all powers and delights,
outstripping limited achievement in any one, to sway
mankind. 109 — Poetry shall be his instrument,
whereby to mould humanity. 110—Called upon to
poetise, Sordello finds that something reached by
song, not song itself, is his desire. 110, 111—Naddo's
good stupidity comments on Sordello. 111, 112—
As for Sòrdello, his fictions so strike the Mantuans,
that he fears being spoilt for his lofty aims by their
flattery. 113, 114—Sordello makes of spoken Italian
a literary language,[1] but greater difficulty lies in
adapting perception to the slow reconstruction of
words. He takes comfort from thinking that, himself
above his poetry, he, not it, is the vital concern, 115
—but a blow comes when he finds people do not see

[1] See Dante, *De Volgari Eloquio*, I. 15.

Sordello in Sordello's characters. 116—This audience is no better than his childish one. 117—Years pass, Sordello's 'Man-portion' is content with ignoble rewards, is sundered from his still intact Poet-half. 118—Each cancels the other's action. 121, 122—He is matched with poetasters, and 'Naddo' makes his vulgar suggestions for Sordello's (and here Browning's) attainment of success. 124—Distracted for want of a comprehensive point of view, Sordello alternately finds body alone and soul alone impracticable. 125—Adelaide of Vicenza dying, Ecelin seeks to marry his children to Guelfs. 126—Taurello, apprised, hastens to prevent this, but only Palma is still *unGuelfed*. 127-130—Sordello is urged to greet Taurello with song, but, disappointed of poetry's second lure, he retreats to Goito to devise some new foot-hold.

Book the Third. 134, 135—The river's flooding rouses Sordello from artificial lethargy, through realising that though Nature repeats itself, Man's opportunities do not. Sordello has squandered his one chance of love, pleasure, esteem. His own development, not these, was his desire; now he sees that development is only attainable through experience of life. 139, 140—He wasted his Mantuan life, he now will gather up the fragments, act and live, however imperfectly. 141—Palma summons Sordello to Verona, 142-144—and we have returned to the night glanced at in Book the First. 144-146—Palma confesses her need of and attraction to Sordello. 147-150—Sketching the scheming Adelaide, Palma describes her death-bed, Ecelin's retirement, and her own ambition, stimulated by Salinguerra, to expand Adelaide's Ghibellin policy. 152—To enmesh Richard, Palma's betrothal to him has still to be assumed. 153— Palma has come for Ecelin's warrant to Taurello to act. That failing, she chooses this occasion to declare herself. Her interests are henceforth indivisible from Sordello. 154—Fate[1] has placed action within Sordello's grasp. Henceforth mankind shall be

> "by him themselves made act,
> Not watch Sordello acting each of them."

156—Like a magician leaving his magic tree, Browning—at Venice—enters upon a 'Digression' till the end of the Book. He exalts Poet Sordello, beyond and larger than his art, above Poet Eglamor, whose art is his sole existence. 158—The greater poet, like the sailor, willingly describes his voyages, but, at the first opportunity, departs on new explorations. These, not describing them, constitute his life. 159—Browning by preference chooses a sin and sorrow-burdened auditor, 163—since evil is inevitable in life, and each human being latently loves good though apparently following evil. 164—But false professors of relief, begone! Browning, calling himself an awkward Moses, smites the true rock. 165—He vindicates his poetry as that of a probationary world. 166-168—Three classes of poets exist; a specimen from each is given. 169—

[1] See p. 64.

Sordellos and Salinguerras are separate entities as yet, 171—and Sordello's nature is designated 'a god's germ.'

Book the Fourth. 173, 174 — The ransoming envoys and Legate appear in Ferrara. The city has suffered from Guelfs and Ghibellins. 176, 177—The League's delegates discuss the ill-reputed House of Ecelo and the ravages around. 178, 179 — The garden and statues are described that Taurello raised for his wife, Retrude, Heinrich's kinswoman. 180— Sordello, arrived with Palma, is startled by to-day's experience into finding humanity larger than he thought. 182—Behind their representatives, press the masses. To fulfil their dumb demand for happiness, he primarily vows himself. 185—Will Pope or Kaiser help best? 186—He puts this question to Taurello, whose answer cruelly wounds his enthusiasm. As he staggers away, fresh human horrors disclose themselves. 187 — His rhymes, how futile now! 188-190 — Salinguerra, a contrast to Sordello, is musing too. 191-194—His thoughts are occupied with his past, his curious failures in attainment, his old bitter grudge against the Estian Guelfs, his Ghibellin marriage, the Guelf routing of himself and Ecelin from Vicenza. 195 — Since then, he has merged himself in Ecelin. 196, 197 — Taurello's accomplishments are worn lightly, for utilitarian, not ideal, ends. 198-203—Ecelin's decline and present monkish dotage are indeed far from that delirious night they fled and fired Vicenza, when Elcorte[1]

---

[1] See p. 104.

saved Adelaide and her newborn babe, while Retrude and hers . . . . Taurello recalls Heinrich's promise of the Prefecture of Lombardy, to-day redeemed in the Imperial rescript. 204—Shall Taurello wear Friedrich's badge? 206—Shall young Ecelin? Taurello returns to more immediate questions. 207 — A marvellous simile illustrates the cool practicality that disperses his reverie. 208—Sordello begs Palma to explain Ghibellin ethics. 209—Her unsatisfactory reply makes him ask if Guelfs are better, or as bad; whether either party loves the people. 210—Is there a third and nobler cause whereby he can serve man? The deeds of Crescentius (A.D. 998) suggest the worth and meaning of Rome. Rome shall typify man's cause, and rebuilding Rome, Sordello's work.

Book the Fifth. 214—Reactionary disgust at the brutishness of the masses overtakes Sordello. 215-218—His visionary Rome disappears. But an encouragement Sordello needs is given in the form of an eloquent enlargement of the saying that Rome was not built in a day. Progress, in poetry or social welfare, comes of collective, associated efforts. 219 - 222 — Strength (as Charlemagne and his successors) emerged first, slowly followed by Knowledge (as Hildebrand and his). From these, new combinations arose, and their full developments, in which Knowledge ever tends to supersede Strength, are yet to come. 223—Each advance, however small, must be secure and thorough. Sordello may shirk service if he chooses, but can he now? 224, 225—

His question rather is, how can he, pricked on to real effort by comprehending real misery, give Crescentius-like help? 226—By inspiring action in—Taurello Salinguerra! Indifferently well received, 227, 228—he adjures Taurello to turn Guelf (since Guelfs and Rome favour the multitude). Alas, Sordello looks for applause too, and his speech is vitiated by consciousness of merit, by self-display. Half-rhetorical, half-earnest, it gains Taurello's contempt for 'poesy.' 228-235—Self-scorn is harder, and goaded to his best, Sordello forgets himself, and with infinite nobleness vindicates the Poet, while condemning himself. 236—The Poet, finest effluence of Knowledge, is, and will be, earth's king, exalted in degree, but resembling other men in kind. Sordello's vision of poetry distinguishes as types Dante, Shakspere, and the poet of a later age, and ends with rejoicing, 237-239—which may be Browning's or Sordello's, on his individual advance in securing comprehension and sympathy. 240—Taurello is stirred, not moved Sordello's way. He sanctions Palma's love, recounts his negative views concerning the badge, 242—which, half instinctively, half capriciously, he throws round Sordello, pronouncing him Romano's Head. 243—Emotion at high tide, Palma tells Goito's secret. 244-246—Divining that Taurello's supremacy depended on an heir, Adelaide unscrupulously concealed the fact of his child's surviving that Vicenza flight, in jealousy for her boy. Thus, Sordello, called Elcorte's son, is Salinguerra's. 247-249—Taurello's ambition revives; they shall be independently powerful. 251—A wonderful picture is presented where the exultant soldier, alone with Palma, describes their conquering future. 253—A sound above arrests them and the end approaches.

Book the Sixth. 255—Fate, conscious of a crisis, pauses with Sordello. 256—He becomes aware that his life has lacked the great motive-power, love. 257—Without its task-master no life is effective. Some external motive must inspire Action, which is a result, never a cause. 259, 260—Sophistry intervenes. Does a Sordello transcend, originate law? Does he not serve men by ministering to himself? 261—He can do much for himself, little for the race. 262—Conscience suggests the value of that little, now exemplified in foregoing the Prefecture. 263-267—Temptation suggests every specious reason against doing so. Sordello's problem is hard. 268—Is not Sordello's complete bliss more than a set-off against an infinitesimal diminution of joy divided among the crowd? 269—He longs for life. Perhaps his world is made to quench his thirst for life. 270, 271—If so, how great the error of refusing the cup for the sake of some future one, and all the while uncertain if he serves mankind perceptibly by his denial! 272—'Life!' why have 'sage, champion, martyr,' relinquished it then? He has not their secret. To glean, not forego, experience ever seemed duty to him. 273, 274—Diving deeper into truth, Sordello perceives that Soul and Eternity are hard to reconcile with their necessary instruments, Matter and Time. Joy comes of their correlation, Sorrow comes when Soul overinforms Matter. 275—Body is short-lived, Soul eternal, and Soul seeking to reconcile their difference only finds Body . . . dead. Such is now the case with Sordello. 277—But the disproportion between Soul and Body may be accepted and used more wisely than Sordello knew. 279—He needed God, and especially God in Christ. 279—Sordello's last act is to spurn selfishness, to tread underfoot the badge. Yet an insect understands adapting means to ends better than Sordello did. 280, 281—Salinguerra, his ambition again cut short, marries Ecelin's youngest daughter and is reabsorbed into Romano. 282—The Ghibellins aggrandise, 283— but Taurello at eighty is in easy imprisonment in Venice. 285—Ecelin III. and Alberic deserve their violent ends. 286—Browning retains a tenderness for Eglamor, 287—quotes later Sordello traditions, 288—and describes Sordello's divided Will as a fatal disease. Yet, after all, Eglamor is a singing lark, Sordello a higher being though undeveloped, a child who sings "unintelligible words," but all the while "up and up goes he."

This briefest of surveys ignores *Sordello's* encrusted gems; for instance, of quaint adornment, as that wherein the 'Soldan's pining daughter' figures (p. 129), vivid description, as of the scene and mood when Palma leaves Sordello (p. 64), and wondrous portraiture, as of Ecelin's daughters,

> "sly and tall
> And curling and compliant" (p. 62).

After *Sordello*, it will be found that Browning changes his hero, and in Sordello himself we trace the change in process. Browning's characters will always be full of thought, but hereafter the thoughts will be about life, not about self.

Pippa Passes; A Drama, 1841 (Vol. III.), is simpler to understand than the foregoing poems, and the help of a detailed summary is not needed towards enjoying the beauty of it and sounding the depth. *Pippa Passes* is alternately idyllic and tragic. Fourteen-year-old Pippa, a silk-winder, begins her one annual holiday by deciding that during the day she will fancy herself each of the four people she deems happiest in Asolo. Each is loved, and she is lonely, but Pippa's hymn, the key-note of the piece, declares the service of all God's children to be equally valuable in His sight. So it comes about that Pippa, as she wanders round Asolo through morning, noon, evening, and night, unconsciously influences the lives of those four she is fancying herself, by her songs and the goodness and innocence they breathe. Ottima, Phene, Luigi, Monsignor, all owe to Pippa redemption from evil. Each of the day's four groups is at some crisis of character and action, in which temptation would conquer, but for the better inspiration coming from the passing words. With beautiful 'dramatic justice,' in the last case, Monsignor's, Browning makes Pippa the unwitting instrument of her own protection.

The *Morning* of *Pippa Passes* is in many respects the most powerful scene in Browning. At first, Ottima and her lover attempt a forced disregard of their crime, but vainly. Sebald, the more accessible to remorse, will not drink the red wine, for to his horrified imagination it looks like Luca's blood. It is the crowning ingratitude of having slain the man who was good to him that tortures Sebald. Ottima tries to make him face the deed more coolly, and seems winning him away from conscience, when Pippa passes singing, and Sebald's saving recoil is completed by her words. Ottima looks no longer superb, but frightful, and he loathes her. Her replies to his bitter words are intensely dramatic in their eloquent shortness. When Sebald instinctively feels that death is the only expiation for the law of life he has outraged, even Ottima rises out of her selfishness. Buried conscience revives in

"kill me,
Mine is the whole crime. Do but kill me."

Her one impulse now is to protect Sebald, and that being impossible, to die with him. In *Pippa Passes* and *A Soul's Tragedy* Browning introduces prose scenes as suitable to unimaginative characters.

When Pippa passes singing at noon, the crisis, if less tremendous, is more touching. The lofty, pure-minded sculptor, tricked and humiliated, is dismissing the bride who has been palmed upon him, when a new idea, suggested by Pippa's song, strikes him. Instead of being the raised in love, shall he not be the raiser, the sculptor of a moral Galatea, of this woman 'with the new soul'? So the diviner spark is elicited from *this* apparently hopeless love.

The young patriot, Luigi, who acts from impulse and feelings, believes it his duty to assassinate the Austrian ruler, therefore his temptation lies in being dissuaded from his resolve. His mother works on him to desist, through her love and the remembrance of a young girl, Chiara. Here the most beautiful of Pippa's songs interposes, to remind Luigi that, for the sake of the ideal 'king,' he must destroy the 'Python' at Vienna. The poetry of *Noon*, especially that exquisite passage beginning 'last year's sunsets, and great stars,' has the pre-eminence, but the motive of action is not equal to the others. The meanings assigned to duty and temptation are fictitious, and the benefit of Pippa's song is accidental, for only owing to an official blunder is Luigi's departure for Vienna unmolested.

In Part IV., the little silk-winder being found to be Monsignor's niece, whose inheritance he has wrongfully enjoyed, the deadly temptation to have her made away with is dissipated by the sweet words of passing Pippa.

"Suddenly God took me"

is the closing line. Hearing this, the Bishop, who

was to have let a devilish man take the unconscious singer, can bear the hideous idea no longer. Lastly we see Pippa back in her bed-room, babbling to her martagon lily, never dreaming how near she has come to-day to the inner lives of Asolo's Four chosen Ones. In this play Browning impresses what Pippa cannot know, *i.e.* how mistaken an estimate we may form of the happiness of others, and how little the appearance of well-being may mean, for was not the mill-girl happier than the people she fancied 'Happiest'?

King Victor and King Charles; A Tragedy, 1842 (Vol. III.), is a page from Sardinian history. In 1730, Victor Amadeus, first King of Sardinia, abdicated in favour of his son, Charles Emanuel. In 1731, he attempted to resume the crown. The only divergence from fact is in the close of the play. In Charles, Browning depicts a man whose master-motive is the sense of responsibility. His character, set over against his father's, represents the moral triumph of honesty and candour over intrigue and guile. Inferior to Victor in mental calibre, Charles attests Browning's line in *La Saisiaz*,

"Weakness never needs be falseness."

First Year, 1730. King Victor. Part I. We are first acquainted with the stunted life dragged on by Prince Charles and his wife, Polyxena, in Victor's court. Ignored till his brother's death made him heir, Charles has ever been sneered at and insulted by his father and the minister, D'Ormea. When the tragedy opens, their 'policy' has exposed Victor to such threatened vengeance from Spain and Austria, who have been disgracefully deceived, and from an overtaxed people, mad with wrongs, that he decides to escape by passing on the crown, with its responsibilities, to his son. Charles is at first ignorant of the intended abdication and its causes, and he takes D'Ormea's self-interested dissuasions from kingship as conveying his father's wish that he should retire from the succession. Sickened of painful and fruitless efforts to cope with statepapers, Charles determines to forestall matters by voluntarily retiring. Part II. D'Ormea seeks to dissuade Victor from abdication, knowing what ruin the abrupt change means for him, but the second-rate knave looks in vain for consideration from the abler one. When Charles enters, his own intended resignation gives him nerve and self-respect that surprise Victor. Charles accepts the pilotage of the state—to Polyxena's dismay. She suspects all Victor does, and judges his abdication a temporary ruse. Already, the firm dignity of Charles's view of his new responsibility disconcerts his father. D'Ormea tries to leave the ship he believes sinking, but is retained by Charles, whose moral uprightness is associated with a hesitant weakness, which his wife's stronger mind strives to correct. Second Year, 1731. King Charles. Part I. In a year, Victor is weary of retirement, and Charles having supplanted the crooked ways of the last administration by right dealing, and re-established the realm in respect and content, the crown again offers attractions to the perfidious ex-king, now 'Count Tende.' He steals to Rivoli Palace, and his monologue there is the finest study in the drama. Till Victor appeared, Charles had not altogether believed him capable of this perjured close to his strategical abdication. Victor of course shows himself utterly ignorant of the depths of faithfulness and responsibility in the nature of Charles, who however ignores his father's real design, and even attempts to screen it. Part II. Victor's conspiracy, spied upon by D'Ormea, approaches its climax. Charles still mistrusts D'Ormea, (whom he has made a better man) and partly to test him, partly because he will not, in the last resort, resign the realm without doing his utmost duty in its defence, he insists on putting the minister's cautions to extreme proof. The great, unwavering conscience of one of Browning's noblest women comes out in Polyxena's admonition to Charles to live out the dim and difficult duty of supporting the crown. To Charles's anguish, D'Ormea has persevered, and Victor is brought in, a prisoner. This unseemly degradation is too much for the son's instincts, and he returns the crown to his father. But the old, fraudful life is played out, and, acknowledging Charles's superiority, Victor dies. His last word is tantamount to an avowal that his abdication proved the only real good of his reign.

Dramatic Lyrics (1842) was the title of *Bells and Pomegranates*, No. III. The sixteen poems are now dispersed under various headings, as indicated below.

Cavalier Tunes (Vol. VI.) (I. *Marching Along*, II. *Give a Rouse*, III. *Boot and Saddle*, originally called *My Wife Gertrude*), are splendid presentations of the royalist spirit. 'Young Harry' is Sir Henry Vane the younger.

My Last Duchess (Vol. V.) (with *Count Gismond*, originally called *Italy and France*) ushers in the long series of Browning's monologues. The Duchess seems a first sketch for the heroine of *The Flight of the Duchess*. Note the significant bronze 'Neptune, taming a sea-horse.' Such a Neptune Ferrara's Duke would fain have been.

Count Gismond—Aix in Provence (Vol. V.) is a fine 'impression' of mediævalism, with its absolute faith in ordeals by battle. Among the fine touches is that foreshadowing of Pompilia and Caponsacchi in the twelfth stanza.

Incident of the French Camp (Vol. V.) (with *Soliloquy of the Spanish Cloister*, originally called *Camp (French) and Cloister (Spanish)*), vividly realises an instance of his 'children's' enthusiasm for Napoleon.

Soliloquy of the Spanish Cloister (Vol. VI.) is a 'study' of the ingenuities of envy, hatred, malice, and uncharitableness.

In a Gondola (Vol. V.) is a lyric story of love, every fantasy of which is dogged by tragic destiny. The dusk villainy of the 'Three,' *her* friends who for some reason are *his* foes, gives the fit quietus. *In a Gondola* is peerless in lovely grace.

Artemis Prologizes (Vol. IV.) is a fragment of an unwritten large work. While her ministrant, Æsculapius, tends and revives the slaughtered Hippolytus, Artemis recounts his death, its cause, and what potency bore him to her woods and now awaits his restoration.

Waring (Vol. V.) is a fantasia on the disappearance from London of a modern man. The fascination of mystery hangs about the character, departure, and subsequent doings of Waring. The simile of the unflattered lady, by which Waring's friend illustrates his memory of him, evinces the very genius of sympathy. Browning speaks in *Waring* of a certain March as the month when

"small birds said to themselves
What should soon be actual song,"

a lovely infusion of imagination into observation.

Rudel to the Lady of Tripoli (Vol. IV.) reads like some crusading romaunt, and may well be called *Queen Worship*, under which title it and *Cristina* originally appeared.

Cristina (Vol. VI.) contains Browning's extremest statement of love being life's paramount object. It is to be taken to some extent dramatically.

Browning condemns those who allow worldly considerations to quench confessed and mutual love. Stanzas 3 and 4 are particularly fine, apart from their context.

Johannes Agricola in Meditation (Vol. IV.) expresses the ecstatic satisfaction of some mediæval believer in predestination. Johannes 'glorifies' God by blaspheming His reason and goodness.

Porphyria's Lover (Vol. V.) describes how a man strangled his love, in the insane idea of so preserving her passion for him from deflection. The power of the poem lies in its imaginative circumstances, and in the madman's view of his deed as natural and virtuous.

Through the Metidja to Abd-El-Kadr (Vol. VI.) records, in mimetic measure, a desert ride. It breathes an Eastern's fanatic mysticism.

The Pied Piper of Hamelin; a Child's Story (Vol. V.) is all fun and frolic, with an indisputable 'moral' tacked on.

The Return of the Druses; A Tragedy, 1843 (Vol. III.), illustrates Browning's interest in race differences. Arab character is throughout the drama contrasted with 'Frank' or European. The action ('Time — 14—, Place — an Islet of the Southern Sporades'), occupies half a day, every hour of which is surcharged with incident and excitement.

Act I. begins with the dawn of the great day when the island's Christian Prefect, the scourge of the Druse exiles, is to be slain by Djabal, and the re-incarnation of their Khalif God (Hakeem) to take place in the person of Djabal, who will lead his tribe under Venetian convoy home to Lebanon. Loys, Djabal's Breton friend, knows no more of these secrets than the yet uninitiated among the Druses. If he did, he would utterly scout the notion of Djabal's divinity. To-day Loys returns from Rhodes with other means of delivering the Druse tribe from their oppression. Act II. Djabal's inherited wrongs and unique rank marked him for leadership from the first. Anael, his betrothed, unconsciously lit in him the enthusiasm of believing himself the latent Hakeem. Once a genuine delusion, the assumption has grown almost unbearable to him. It has degraded a noble nature to the lying tricks of the impostor, hourly more difficult to abandon. We cannot sympathise with Djabal if we judge him purely by European standards. It is the mingling of Frank influences with the native Orientalism of his character that furnishes the key to his morbid development. Anael, a typical theocrat, with her burning Eastern heart, unconsciously feels, by love's instinct, that Djabal is merely a man, even such a one as Loys. This, far from shaking her loyalty, only oppresses her with a sense of terrible unworthiness in herself, which prevents her from recognising the coming God, and renders her unfit to share in Djabal's 'elevation.' Act III. To wipe out what she considers her disgrace, Anael meditates some tremendous sacrifice, some 'deed' which shall absolve her. Almost before her interview with Loys (p. 207), we feel that she is nerving herself, and has donned the Druse weapon in order to forestall Djabal in slaying the Prefect. She shrinks from it, but she will do it. Act IV. Anael's words, when she emerges from the Prefect's chamber and tells Djabal what she has done, are thrilled with horror. The utter contrast between the Prefect's self-gratulation over his safety, and his instantaneous death—with the groan Loys takes for laughter—is intensely dramatic. When Djabal, overwhelmed by Anael's deed, which truthfulness of his would have averted, does at last confess to her his deceit, her momentary revulsion, and then her faithful love, not untouched with gladness, and combined with fearless resolution to have the truth told, lead up to the last touch of her devotedness. The torrent of her contempt at Djabal's refusal to confess his falseness to their people forces her to denounce him to the Nuncio. Act V. When, at the end, love, pity, and patriotism wring from her a last offering, the dying cry of *Hakeem*,[1] that turns the tide of the fickle mob for Djabal, we feel that all the poetry of the play concentres in Anael. Loys, the knight-novice, with his noble love for Anael, is a brave, manly figure. The Nuncio, sent by the Patriarch of the Eastern Church, is, whatever his corruption, at least no coward. He is a specimen of Browning's favourite type of a worldly ecclesiastic. The same general features belong to him as to Monsignor in *Pippa*

[1] Compare Desdemona's "*Nobody*; *I myself.*"

Passes, Ogniben in *A Soul's Tragedy*, and Bishop Blougram. Khalil, Anael's brother, is Anael with the ever-womanly left out. His appeal to Djabal to restore his sister to life is piteously poignant. The swift fire of fanaticism inherent in Asiatics, the clashing ideas and interests of various peoples, and the mob's unfailing greed and unruliness form a rich and picturesque background.

A Blot in the 'Scutcheon; A Tragedy, 1843 (Vol. IV.), is the one play of Browning's which gives an impression of painful and unconquerable dissonance between plot and treatment. In *Romeo and Juliet* and *Faust*, every step of the march of events is inevitable, with that inevitableness which is the life of drama, but from which Mertoun's wronging of Mildred stands absolutely apart. The central subject of *A Blot in the 'Scutcheon* is inadequately motived. Mertoun's boyish dread of Tresham, which he strives to plead in extenuation, would be a wretched coward's excuse, and the extreme youth of both lovers, also pleaded in extenuation, would as such be repulsive, did we not feel that both pleas are unreal. Taking the facts of her story as we find them, the Mildred of Act I. is untrue to nature as no character of Browning's ever was before or since. The enchanting beauty of the poetry is heavily handicapped, and the impression the drama leaves is one of staginess, slightness, and ineffectualness, almost as though the planned-out work of an inferior writer had been bequeathed to Browning to make the best of.

Act I., Scenes 1 and 2 describe the state visit of

Earl Mertoun to sue for the hand of Mildred Tresham. The diamond-witted Guendolen discovers the flaw in his suit, viz. his absence of anxiety to be furthered in the lady's own good graces. All his diffidence is expended on Mildred's brother, Lord Tresham. This, and old Gerard's unexplained trouble, are our first intimation that all is not well. In Tresham we see a man of two ideas, fraternal affection and family pride. The expected canker in the rose proves to be the previous illicit love of Mertoun and Mildred, with the piteous story of which Scene 3 acquaints us. Mertoun's tender devotion cannot allay Mildred's remorse. The glaring falseness of their betrothal is torture to her deep, earnest nature. In Act II., the retribution, which Mildred rightly knew was inherent in the sin, begins to be accomplished. Tresham learns that the sister he deemed so peerless' receives an unknown, secret visitor. Entreated to explain, Mildred attempts no palliation, only refuses to tell her lover's name. Tresham accepts a hushed, stained future for himself and her, but first bids her dictate to him the Earl's dismissal. This she refuses to do. Wrought past silence at such crowning depravity, and too headstrong to guess the truth, Tresham calls his brother and Guendolen, and before them curses Mildred. With womanly chivalry, Guendolen interposes, and showing the pearl side of her character in refusing to believe the worst, presently guesses that it was Mertoun's name Mildred concealed. Act III. At midnight, in the avenue, Tresham comes upon the destroyer of his sister's honour. Challenged to make known who he is, Mertoun discloses himself. Tresham, inexpressibly disgusted at his perfidy, without allowing him to speak, bids him draw. Mertoun suffers himself to be mortally wounded, and falls. The non-resistance and the upturned, boyish face give Tresham's anger pause. Pardoning and pardoned, he bitterly rues his cruel haste, but too late to save the life he has taken. In Scene 2, Tresham is with Mildred. She quickly divines from what deed he comes, and, dying herself, grants forgiveness to her brother. Tresham, whose eyes sorrow and repentance have unbandaged, sees and understands the purity beneath the blot, the life more sacred than the 'scutcheon. Nothing is left him, he feels, but to follow Mertoun and Mildred, and as the poison he has taken ends his life, he reminds those who hang over him that only disaster and failure come when a man assumes God's prerogative of judgment and requital.

Colombe's Birthday; A Play, 1844 (Vol. IV.), is a drama of which the story, only imaginatively historical, exactly suits the development of Browning's special methods. It gives scope to the all-pervasive unconventionality and the creating of mental zigzags and surprises that characterise his 'fundamental brain-work.'

Act I. Prince Berthold, abetted by Pope and kings, has just sent in his claim to his young cousin Colombe's Duchy, under Salic law. The few courtiers who have not openly deserted Colombe's sinking fortunes are disputing which shall present the disconcerting document. Of the self-interested crew, Gaucelme is most, Guibert least corrupt. Guibert has just expressed supreme contempt for the brutish People, when, from the almost empty vestibule, a suitor, Valence, the 'advocate' of Cleves, forces his way in. He pleads Cleves' woes to his old debtor, Guibert, as a means towards laying Cleves' petition before Colombe. His severely simple negative to the courtiers' question whether rumour bruits Colombe's coming ruin convinces Gaucelme that the right man to present Berthold's missive — as the price of approach to Colombe—is Valence. Ignorant of the contents, Valence accedes. Act II. The Duchess marks the scanty attendance at her audience, but as yet no report of Berthold's entrance has reached her. Valence, who saw Colombe a year ago and loved her with a man's love beside a subject's loyalty, advances and describes his townsmen's sufferings, at the same time presenting Berthold's requisition. Colombe reads it, and with dignified gentleness prepares to resign her coronet. Valence flashes his indignation at Guibert for his trickery, and, turning to Colombe, begs her to shake off this mist of courtiers between herself and her real subjects, and remain Duchess for the People's sake. Colombe, inspired by enthusiasm, congenial but hitherto unknown, defies Berthold, dismisses her courtiers, and takes Valence for counsellor. Act III. Berthold, arrived, is discussing with Melchior his past and present position regarding this step towards his end, the Empire. He treats the servile courtiers with sardonic irony, till Guibert, showing a grain of conscience, or of shame at being inferior to Valence, utters Colombe's defiance. Berthold, startled, even pleasurably piqued, by Colombe's daring, makes way as she enters talking to Valence. Colombe, because she feels she has been a 'play-queen,' is again inclining to relinquish her sway. Berthold affects to regard the denial of his claim as her friends' doing, not hers. Valence, with deep, chivalrous enthusiasm, which transcends Berthold's princely politeness, dispels this, and, while describing Colombe as alone, describes her People as hers to live or die. Berthold, entertaining a new idea, forbears further discussion, gives Valence his credentials, and withdraws. The courtiers decide that Colombe and Valence love each other, and retire to shape a suitable policy. Colombe, best of disciples, though not of solitary learners—a true woman—leaves Valence to decide her course. He is torn between love and duty, love urging him to lower Colombe's rank, and duty to guide her towards beneficent rule. But with the genius of conscience, he determines to judge regardlessly of consequence. Act IV. The courtiers' scheme is to win Berthold's gratitude by apprising him that if Colombe marries the advocate, she forfeits her Duchy to himself, the next heir. Meantime Valence has found Berthold's claims incontrovertible. He is deprecating his own consequent joy, when

Berthold enters to say that he proposes to make assurance doubly sure by wedding Colombe—a message he charges Valence to give her. When Colombe next appears, she is almost happily contemplating private liberty, and Valence's task is all the harder. In a speech of nobly imaginative insight, he depicts the true greatness of the imperial career, then tenders her Berthold's proposal. The thought of an imperial lover flatters her, but Valence rightly deducts love from the proposal. His reason asked, it is, he answers, love's instinct. The idea that Valence loves is importunate and engrossing (so we watch Colombe's own love dawning), and bit by bit it comes out whom he loves. At present the declaration hurts Colombe: the morning's service then was love, not loyalty, and nothing is what it seems. Act V. To Berthold, the fulfilment of ambition is an absorbing art, loved for the skill's sake. When he states his proposal to Colombe, he explicitly disclaims sentiment, proffering her his Empire to be,—and regard. The courtiers here spring their mine, winning scant thanks from Berthold. What they effect is to hasten Colombe's decision. Neither Berthold nor his friend can conceive the lady refusing the Empire, and Valence trembles. But love beckons sweet Colombe, and she resigns her Duchy in order to bestow herself upon Valence. Berthold half regretfully admires her conduct, acknowledging the Duchy she so easily relinquishes to be far more necessary to himself than to her. Guibert follows the lady to Ravestein and his former comrades are promised a sufficiently penal future.

Dramatic Romances and Lyrics (1845), was the title of *Bells and Pomegranates*, No. VII. The contents are now distributed under other titles.

How they brought the Good News from Ghent to Aix (Vol. VI.), that glorious 'stirrup-piece,' is popular wherever English is spoken, and Roland is the prince of poetry's horses.

Pictor Ignotus (Vol. IV.) is one of Browning's Art poems and turns on an artist's personal problem. Rather than lower his refined ideal to the vulgarity of picture-buyers and the mart, the 'unknown painter,' shrinking into himself, chooses to paint cold and lifeless altar-pieces. He gives up conceiving pictures such as Rafael's, and sacrifices the happiness and stimulus of such praise and love as met the work of Cimabue.

The Italian in England (Vol. V.) (originally called *Italy in England*), is a Lombard exile's reminiscence of a desperate expedient, during Metternich's administration, which brought him rescue at the hands of a peasant girl. He lives to recall her generous courage and to labour anew for Italy.

The Englishman in Italy (Vol. V.) (originally called *England in Italy*), is Browning's one purely descriptive poem. 'The Englishman' tells over to a child listener details and peculiarities of the nature and natural life of the Sorrento Plain and Bay of Naples. *Lasagne* is the flat, broad macaroni. The English

Corn-laws (repealed in 1846) are compared to the withering, oppressive Scirocco.

The Lost Leader (Vol. VI.), records the desertion by a certain poet of the cause of liberty and progress. The last four lines recommend him to justify his instruction by doughty fighting, though for the new party, opposing and menacing the old. Time will reconvert him, and then—for he is still loved—God will pardon him and reunite him to his first allies.

The Lost Mistress (Vol. VI.) is a man's regretful acceptance of friendship where love existed previously. Stanza 2 is a delicious nature note.

Home-Thoughts from Abroad (Vol. VI.) sketches English April and May. Browning's works contain no more magical touches than the words describing the 'buttercups' and 'wise thrush.'

Home-Thoughts, from the Sea (Vol. VI.) records a noble question, nobly answered by Browning in his gift of poetry to England.

The Bishop orders his Tomb at Saint Praxed's Church (Vol. IV.) (originally called *The Tomb at Saint Praxed's*), is a marvellous piece of craftsmanship. After reading it, one never again hears the 'blessed mutter' in a Roman church, or goes round the ecclesiastics' monuments of *cipollino* or *nero-antico* without recalling the voluptuous pagan of the Renaissance, who implores his 'nephews' for good marble, good carving, and Ciceronian Latin. '*Elucescebat*' ('he shone forth' or 'was notable') should be 'elucebat.' The Bishop derides Ulpian's dog-latin.

Garden Fancies (Vol. VI.) I. *The Flower's Name* is a lover's delicate rhapsody. II. *Sibrandus Schnafburgensis* is the portentous name of the writer of a dull and solemn book, a reader's merry revenge on which the poem narrates. The spider 'with arms akimbo' is an amusing touch of actuality.

The Laboratory (Vol. VI.) (with *The Confessional* called *France and Spain*), is a vivid picture of the intense, scorching jealousy of an unscrupulous woman, who flourished when poisoning was fashionable. In a speaking picture, Browning makes us see the keeper of the poison shop and his fair, evil customer.

The Confessional (Vol. VI.) is the desperate outcry of an unhappy girl, whom a priest inveigled, under false pretences, into telling the secrets of her lover, a malcontent. Two days later, she saw her lover executed. She has herself been incarcerated and tortured for her impotent denunciation of priestly treachery.

The Flight of the Duchess (Vol. V.) is the enchantingly fantastic narrative of an ardent, natural young girl's immurement in artificial surroundings and among unloving people. The death-in-life becoming impossible, she escapes, under the influence of a wondrous crone, the Gipsies' Queen. The descriptions of Moldavia, the 'middle-age-manners-adapter' Duke, the crafts of the gipsies, and the Duchess's departure are particularly fresh and romantic. The lulling, stimulating words the gipsy croons over the Duchess are open to wide interpretation. Their didactic mysticalness is effectively contrasted with the rough and ready style of the huntsman who tells the story. In this poem, Browning first speaks of the distinct happiness of age in restful retrospect, the harvesting of ripened memories, that happy, characteristic view of *By the Fireside*, *Rabbi Ben Ezra*, and other poems.

Earth's Immortalities (Vol. VI.) reminds us how oblivion swallows fame, and how love passes too, and, despite its febrile promise of 'for ever,' becomes as forgotten as June is in autumn's snows.

Song (Vol. VI.) is a lover's impassioned demand of praise for his lady, who is too dear to him for his own praising.

The Boy and the Angel (Vol. V.) is a kind of legend of how Gabriel took Theocrite's place, that Theocrite might be Pope. Both angel and boy found their mistake, for God missed the 'little human praise.' Each returned to his proper calling, with the chastening knowledge that while all service ranks the same with God, each creature's grace is evinced in acquiescence in the conditions of his own life.

Meeting at Night and *Parting at Morning* (Vol. VI.) (originally called *Night and Morning*), are descriptive and ethical, the second poem implying that as surely as morning brings the sun his task, the privilege and responsibility of life in the world devolve on a man (cp. the first lyric in *Ferishtah*).

Nationality in Drinks (Vol. VI.) (two-thirds of which were originally called *Claret and Tokay*), consists of two lively wine fancies, French and Hungarian, and

a fact concerning Nelson, whose memory is drunk in
'British Beer.'

Saul (Vol. VI.), one of the world's finest poems, is founded on 1 Sam. xvi. 14-23. To arouse the King from his terrible lethargy, David tries all his harp tunes. He begins with the music that folds the sheep, the music that attracts birds and insects, the music of human existence. All these availing little to stir Saul, David sings the joys of living, all concentrated upon Israel's King. Then he turns to life's deeper harmonies, and Saul's great deeds that will never die nor be forgotten. His spirit yearning over Saul in his distress, a great inspiration enters David, and laying aside harp and song, he prophesies, step by step from his own love, which only to die for Saul, if need were, can satisfy, the existence of a similar love in God. It is a tremendous inference, but nothing less is possible, unless the creature is to surpass the creator, and David, enwrapped in vision, sees and knows the Human Love in the Divine Power, the self-sacrificing Christ. As David returns homeward through the night, Nature's voices are hushed with acquiescence in or tremulous in attestation of the new law, the new life. (*Saul* was written in two parts, i.-ix., appearing in 1845, the rest in 1855, among *Men and Women.*)

Time's Revenges (Vol. V.) is a man's bitter reflection on one-sided attraction. His friend's devotion to him, which he repays with contempt, is revenged by his own devouring love for a heartless society woman.

The Glove (Vol. V.) takes up Schiller and Hunt's ballad, treats the theme afresh, and continues it beyond the old conclusion, according to a new view of the conduct of the 'dame' and De Lorge. Instead of taking the well-known superficial, and somewhat brutal, view of the episode, Browning convincingly justifies the lady in putting her knight's professions to the test.

Luria; A Tragedy, 1846 (Vol. VI.), may well be called Browning's favourite drama. The character of Luria, an absolutely original creation without historical basis, is unmatched in literature. Luria shares with Othello the fervour of the Oriental, as, guileless like him, he is surrounded by Italian craft and guile. Luria is the most utterly unselfish and lofty of men. He loved Florence so much, and was so true to her, that he would perish rather than allow her to be false to him. He died to save Florence from that shame.

Act I. ('Scene—Luria's Camp between Florence and Pisa. Time, 14—.') Puccio, the commander Luria has superseded, is reporting to Braccio, the Florentine Signoria's commissary, how Luria stands prepared for to-day's decisive battle with Pisa. Jealous and carping as his displacement inclines him to be, the honest-natured Puccio cannot forbear testifying to Luria's consummate conduct. This message is never destined to reach Florence. Braccio tears the report as soon as Puccio leaves him, substituting a missive to the effect that as the Pisans are sure to be defeated by Luria, the baseless trial (which has been secretly proceeded with in Florence) and sentence of the Moor may be completed. Braccio's Secretary expostulates, but Braccio has determined Luria's fate. Depending on no evidence, he merely takes dangerous ambition for granted in a successful commander. Florentine captains have ended their career so, and, according to Braccio, it is inevitable, all the more in an alien. Braccio regards, or affects to regard, a Moorish mercenary as a dangerous animal, best treated with faithlessness. Luria, entering, shows by his dalliance with the Florentines' suspicion how unconscious he is of his adored city's treachery. To Luria, the Italian character is extraordinarily fascinating, and trustworthy for its very impassibility. Act II. Domizia, whose House has been uprooted by Florence on charges similar to that now laid against Luria, is an embodied revenge, who is influencing Luria for the moment when, his sentence pronounced, he may rise and, with his worshipping army, crush the ungrateful city. Husain, Luria's friend, strives to make Luria distrust Florence and, this victory won, abjure her service. But Luria's feeling, his Eastern dower, is laid under a spell by Florentine thought, and his one prevision is dread of dismissal when Florence needs her fighter no longer. Tiburzio, Pisa's commander, a generous foe, here appears to offer Luria, not truce, but news and proof of the Signoria's treachery. He invites Luria to join Pisa.. Luria will neither read Braccio's intercepted letter, nor believe the treachery without further test. Incapable of baseness, he cannot imagine but that Florence will acquit him if he goes on steadily serving her through this critical day. By Act III., the battle is won, and Tiburzio taken prisoner. Luria, who thought this victory would amend all, finds he was mistaken. Braccio admits the existence of the trial, vindicating the city or nation's carelessness of the individual as necessary to the preservation of itself, the type. He disarms Luria's possible appeal to his soldiery, by denominating such an appeal a justification of the Signory's doubts. Hereupon, Tiburzio again beseeches Luria to change masters, and, alone and without followers, take from him his own commandership, in Pisa's name. But Luria plans a different punishment for Florence, viz. continued rectitude in her service, bound, as he believes, to bring surprised recognition, with attendant shame and remorse. Meantime he dismisses Tiburzio, Braccio, and Domizia, assuring them that till the sentence arrives, he remains the officer of Florence. Act IV. Puccio, who reveres Luria, and Husain, who loves him, think his vengeance on Florence, by the double instrument of his and the Pisan army, worthy and inevitable, and Domizia appeals to Luria to take this revenge for very righteousness' sake. Luria, alone again, far from assimilating the others' suggestions, falls to thinking his own meditated 'revenge' too cruel. After all, the Signory, not the People, are false, so why brand these with eternal disgrace for those? Best disappear, his day ended, like the sun of his native land. To save Florence from the consequences of her 'strange mistake,' he swallows a slow poison. Act V. Luria explains to Puccio how to conclude the campaign victoriously, when he shall have departed, though not to Pisa, as Puccio thought. Overwhelmed by Luria's magnanimity, Puccio refuses to supersede him, and begs to be allowed to serve him. Jacopo, too, the Secretary, on whom Luria enjoins the task of righting the reputation of Domizia's House, is won from Braccio's equivocal service, and, with his heart's homage, accepts Luria's charge. Next enters Domizia, a changed woman, whom knowledge of Luria has taught that revenge is a poor ambition. She divines that whatever Luria now devises for Florence, is at least

"No brute-like punishment of bad by worse."

Tiburzio has used his liberty to visit Florence and there vindicate, as he well could, Luria's unswerving loyalty. Braccio, too, acknowledges his entire conversion to the truth of the Moor. During their speeches, Luria has gradually grown more silent, till suddenly those present find fulfilled the punishment he prepared (as a punishment, unconsciously) for Florence, his own death. Nothing can be more beautiful and impressive than Luria's comment at the close of the confession of each of his convertites, that there's another for eternity. Of all the suicides ever read of there was never one more perfectly purged of self than Luria.

A Soul's Tragedy, 1843 (Vol. III.), is a drama, the title of which is ironic, as the chief personage, Chiappino, merely attitudinises.

Act I. Chiappino is, with Eulalia, awaiting the return of Luitolfo, Eulalia's affianced lover, who has gone to the tyrannical Provost to try to obtain some mitigation of the sentence of banishment passed on Chiappino for reviling the Provost and Provostship. The graceless ingrate, Chiappino, employs the hour in sneering down Luitolfo to Eulalia, and professing his old love for her. This love he describes as all along unspoken, because choked by the forestalling glibness and hampering 'benefits' of the prosperous Luitolfo. Ill-conditioned in adversity, Chiappino puts an ungenerous construction on Luitolfo's deeds and words and, while vaunting his own depth of feeling, love of liberty, and general superiority, proves himself one who only sympathises with himself. He has just denounced the craven spirit of the Faentines and gibed at Luitolfo's probably magniloquent description of an unsuccessful interview with the Provost, when an agitated knocking is heard. Luitolfo enters, his garments blood-stained. He tells them that, goaded past forbearance, he has struck, and, he believes, killed the Provost. To a man of weak nerve, as Luitolfo is, the reaction from his impulsive deed, with the prospect of torture and death, is stupefying. Chiappino rises to the occasion, and almost is, what he has always considered himself, heroic. He hurries the half-stunned Luitolfo out of the house, with his own travelling gear and route, and then puts on Luitolfo's blood-stained vest. He is in a highly excited state when, the multitude rushing in, the situation is instantly transformed, for they reply to Chiappino's announcement, "I killed the Provost!" by hailing him as their saviour and the destroyer of their oppressor. Before the scene closes, we are prepared for what is to follow, for Chiappino shows that the new delight of applause and popularity are too sweet, coming after such strain, to be immediately relinquished. Act II., a month later, represents Luitolfo, in disguise, mingling with the populace, and hearing that Chiappino, having modified his revolutionary ideas, is about to be made the new Provost. To compose the popular tumult, Ogniben, the Pope's Legate, has come over from Ravenna, where the old Provost is lying wounded but not, as was imagined, killed. Ogniben has quickly taken Chiappino's measure. He is now for a time fooling him to the top of his bent, in order to bring him to the more complete collapse. To this end, in discourse with him, he carries out into glaring extremes Chiappino's sophistical vindications of his inconsistency in accepting the Provostship. At last the wily fisher of men sees Chiappino floundering and gasping in the net. Then, to mortify him more entirely, he coolly remarks, that beside the complete dependence of the new Provost on himself, under Rome, he has another stipulation to make, which is, 'that in case the actual assailant of the late Provost is discovered' . . . a sentence cut short by a disconcerted ejaculation from Chiappino. Hereupon, Ogniben, giving his victim to understand how exactly he is acquainted with his false position, publicly demands to have the actual assailant handed over to justice. To this demand Luitolfo has the courage to respond, whereupon Chiappino, to escape the general hiss of derision, slinks out of Faenza, leaving Ogniben still master of the situation.

Christmas-Eve and Easter-Day, 1850 (Vol. V.), is the name of two imaginative religious poems. The central point of each is the Divinity of Christ, and each narrates a revelation in a vision. The only circumstantial link between the poems is that both visions appeared on the same common.

The speaker in *Christmas-Eve* is a man who has received his religious life from nature, though always recognising Divine Love above it. On this Christmas-Eve, he emerges, on the common's edge, from a dissenting chapel in which he had sheltered from the rain. Disgust at the bigotry, the heat without light, of pastor and flock, drove him out again. The storm is succeeded by a double lunar rainbow, and out of this appears the Figure of Christ, almost as though in response to an intuitive expectation that a yet more solemn splendour was about to be revealed. As in a dream, terrified, not surprised, he seizes the hem of Christ's garment, and is borne along by it to Saint Peter's at Rome, where Christ enters, he following Him. At first, he hesitated to do so, feeling that Christ would not expect him to worship amid so much error. Then he reflects that the love of those worshippers' forefathers is what once dissipated by its spirituality the earthliness of the antique world, and that if their descendants' love is still infantine, it is nevertheless love. Again he is caught up in the vesture, and carried to a Göttingen lecture-hall, where a Professor is disposing of the Myth of Christ. Eliminating Christ's Divinity, the lecturer yet calls for enthusiasm for His intellect and goodness. 'Christ's intellect,' comments the listener, 'is no higher a title to veneration than other men's, and rather the less, on account of His claim to Divinity, supposing Him mere man. On the same supposition, Christ's goodness is no title to worship, for goodness, only differing in degree, is common to all, and God's gift. No; the worshipfulness of Christ lies in His Godship, in the motive of love which that furnishes. It is a matter of personal religion, not of morality. And yet there is something to admire in the untamable instinct of the Professor and his pupils to reverence Christ though robbed of Divinity.' As the speaker poises the qualities of the various forms of religion, we recognise in his purely intellectual toleration a tone of superiority, far from the proselytising partisanship, the humble fellowship with Christ, which the vision has yet to teach him. Suddenly, he finds the garment has quitted his hand, and therefrom he learns his lack of conviction and sincerity. The world is large and many-voiced, but each liver in it has only his one life, and this and what he reads in it of teaching or warning, are his prime concern. A man must make some choice of his own. Once more the robe is in his hand, and he is again inside the chapel, his vision over. The people are as ugly and mean as before, but he feels, and no longer only coldly knows, the earnestness and devotion that transform them. His eyes are changed to recognise the water of life in an earthen vessel, and to drink of it gladly.

The humorous descriptions of people, the exquisite idea of sublimating the vision from the rainbow, the repeated description of the movement of the man carried along by Christ's luminous vesture, form a collection of passages that express the whole gamut of Browning's imaginative genius.

The vision of *Easter-Day* is of the Judgment, the account of it being introduced into a conversation between two friends. The subject of their dialogue is the hardness of realising faith sufficiently to make it the master-motive of actual life. Both acknowledge that the difficulty lies in relinquishing the world's obvious gifts for what is at best only known as a promise. The first speaker, whose opinions are, as we find later, solemnised by his visionary experience, is the more earnest, though by disposition the less hopeful, of the two. They discuss and, on the whole, agree to the necessity of faith as God's touchstone for men. They then pass on to consider faith from man's point of view. What evidences are there to make it tenable? The act of renunciation is not the hardest part, for people are constantly found renouncing the world for some one interest or hobby. Here the friends are divided, the second speaker denying that it is necessary to renounce the world in order to be a Christian. The other describes himself as one who would acknowledge the absolute justice of God's 'blacking out' his 'brief life's pleasantness' for his share in the Crucifixion. For his own part, he cannot ignore the Bible's reiterated command to abjure the world. This being his mind, it is, his friend allows, all-important to him to live up to it. Again the first speaker, recollecting what has been said as to the ease with which many renounce the world for purely earthly pursuits, confesses that in the case of even the most trifling, the renouncer has something to show for his pains. This reflection shakes, though it does not overturn, his faith. His friend chides him for disturbing his easier faith by even suggesting so much doubt. In reply to this, the first speaker disallows the faith that looks for easiness. Not only is such confidence a fool's paradise, but the incessant conflict with uncertainty is (and here he speaks with deeper meaning) actually a boon. It proves that the privilege of probation is still ours, that no after-judgment stagnation has fallen upon us. He will explain his conviction by relating a dread vision he saw on Easter-Eve three years before. He was musing as to whether, if death overtook him then and there, he would fall faithful or faithless. Common Sense stayed him with specious comfort, but still he longed for a day when God's will and his duty might be cleared from doubt. Hardly had he done so, when the sky became alight with fire, and, as the flames spread, linking earth and heaven in one grand conflagration, he heard a voice declare his soul judged and Eternity begun. Then the fire seemed suddenly to burn out, leaving the common dark as before. He fancied himself awaked from a nightmare, till once more he heard the voice and this time saw the awful Figure of Christ. He fell on his face before Him, to hear that, having chosen earth during his life, earth should henceforth be his portion. At first, this did not seem the terrible doom it was. 'Nature,' he cried, 'and its beauties, in these I will joy for ever.' The voice replied that earthly beauty was but a pledge of the plenitude, which, whoso retains the pledge for ever, foregoes. 'Then I choose art,' he responded. 'Choose it,' said the voice. 'Without its soul, its hope, its conscious suggestion of unearthly perfection, the noblest art is worthless.' Despairingly, the man clung to Mind, but even as he did so, he realised the emptiness of a race for knowledge the goal of which is proved a ruin. More deeply yet the voice impressed upon him the use of the former life's paradoxes, its intuitions and ignorance, its spirit and sense, its truth and fable. But the man tried yet another choice, and this time chose love, admittedly only the show of it, yet precious for the memory of what love was. At this, his Judge, instead of relenting, answered, more austerely than ever, that Love was the very thing that had mixed in all his former life's concerns, and yet the very thing he could not believe God capable of was the Love of Christ. Then the man, whose every choice had crumbled, prayed Christ to restore to him the semblance of the old life of uncertainty and probation, for the sake of its hope. At this point, the vision passed away, and he was back in the life he had learned to prize. This is the explanation of his conviction that worldly gifts, accepted for their own sake, are unsatisfying, and that warfare and doubt are precious, compared with what might be.

Men and Women, 1855, is a collection of great short poems, chiefly dramatic monologues. The poems are fifty in number, exclusive of the dedication or *One Word More*. *Men and Women* was published in two volumes, the second commencing at *Andrea del Sarto*, and in the following order.

Love among the Ruins (Vol. VI.) describes the glory and pomp of a long dead capital, as contrasted with the present silence of its site. A pair of lovers keep their tryst in the single turret left standing, and

Browning considers it more worthily occupied than in its proud days.

A Lover's Quarrel (Vol. VI.) recounts how happily and easily two lovers passed their time three months ago (January, 1853) when snow-drifts kept them prisoners. They used to play like children, and it passes the man's comprehension that a word can now have sundered them, nullifying their past. It is the harder to bear with spring coming on. If only it were November, the very bareness and coldness of the world would bring them together in a reconciliation which is very easily imaginable.

Evelyn Hope (Vol. VI.) is a poem of the tenderness and love felt by a man of middle age for a young girl, who dies at sixteen. She was not aware of this love, but she is to be, when she awakens in some other life, and, for remembrance, the man folds a leaf into her hand. *Evelyn Hope* is the poem of the unmarried, and should be read in connection with *Cristina*, as giving the other side of love's shield.

Up at a Villa—Down in the City (Vol. VI.) is an amusing contrast, as drawn 'by an Italian Person of Quality,' between the boredom of his country residence and the alluring but ruinous life 'in the city-square.' The mental calibre of the person of quality is humorously self-revealed.

A Woman's Last Word (Vol. VI.) contains the story of a woman who is striving to conform her ideal to a man's requirements. While sorrowfully acknowledging their mutual misunderstanding, she decides to sink her individuality for the sake of the man's love. To contend with him may imperil love, and is therefore as foolish as if two birds were to quarrel while a hawk was watching them.

Fra Lippo Lippi (Vol. IV.) is first of the great monologues grown out of *My Last Duchess* and the dramas, and is one of Browning's finest poems. It is, among other things, Lippo Lippi's plea for naturalism in art. The biographical materials, as with *Andrea* and *Old Pictures in Florence*, are in Vasari, and to look from his biographies to the poems is a lesson in appreciating imaginative literature. Browning's Friar is a flesh-and-blood reality. He is a man of free and merry manners, whose head got inside a cowl by mistake, and a painter who is keenly observant, and resolute in depicting healthful beauty. The man recruits the painter with the perpetual reminder, amid the monastery's bones and nimbus preachments, that

"The world and life's too big to pass for a dream."

'Hulking Tom' is Masaccio, and 'Brother Lorenzo,' a monk of the order of Camaldoli, is the Don Lorenzo of Vasari.

A Toccata of Galuppi's (Vol. VI.) is a dramatic reverie on eighteenth century Venice. The reverie, taking the form of an imaginary conversation with the dead Venetian composer, is coloured, or rather achromatised, by one of his *capriccios*. Galuppi's music reflects the element of dissatisfaction in the frivolous life around it. The people who liked to listen to it have disappeared and left no trace. Their day was an empty one, and doubtless they deserved extinction. At the same time, it is a painful reflection that all their grace and beauty were so vain.

By the Fireside (Vol. VI.) represents a husband's quiet talk, prospect and retrospect, with his wife. The different epochs of his life are strung, like beads, on a thread of love. Before him lie age and the study of Greek, behind him, youth, Italy, and the declaration of his love, made during an Alpine walk. Every feature of that scene was priceless, and seemed to thrill up to a climax, the spoken word which broke down the barrier between the pair, and tested the man's worth and his life's purpose in one supreme opportunity.

Any Wife to any Husband (Vol. VI.) is a dying woman's lament that a man's constancy to a memory is so much more likely to waver than a woman's would be. She would fain believe that her husband will rank no other woman beside her in his heart, that absence will be no sorer trial to him than it would be to her—but she knows otherwise, and her last word expresses this pathetic certainty.

An Epistle of Karshish (Vol. IV.) relates, from an Arab physician's point of view, the impression made upon him by Lazarus, the raised from the dead. The contrast between the physician's quaint preconceptions and the awe-inspiring uniqueness of Lazarus is most striking. The Jew's belief in his 'curer' being God, has made an extraordinary impression on the other's fervent Eastern nature, albeit Karshish professes to look upon his 'case' from the materialistic standpoint. The realisation of the altered mind and conduct of Lazarus is deeply imaginative.[1] *An Epistle* is charged with Browning's favourite religious evidence, the uses of uncertainty. 'Premature full growth' unmans Lazarus.

Mesmerism (Vol. V.) is a description of a feat of 'willing.' First, the lover wills into his presence the image or simulacrum of the girl he loves, and then, by eager concentration of intent, he draws herself, her real presence, into the room. *Mesmerism* ends with abjuring the use of an uncomprehended, unmeasured power.

A Serenade at the Villa (Vol. VI.) is an instance of Browning's power of absolute fusion of the aspects of nature with the imaginations of a man's heart. The serenader hopes his worshipping words were noted, but fears that his lady only declared his song the last element of tiresomeness in oppressive weather.

My Star (Vol. VI.) is a lover's allegory. His 'star' (a favourite term with Browning for untouched perfectness), having revealed herself to him, no outside commendation of her is needed to ratify his love.[2]

Instans Tyrannus (Vol. V.), like *Time's Revenges*, represents an ugly trait of humanity. Here it is the

[1] Cp. *In Memoriam*, xxxi.
[2] Contrast with this *personal* expression. a *dramatic* passage in opposition to its sentiment in *Fifine at the Fair*, XI. 243-244.

capricious cruelty of some threatening ruler, hating for hating's sake. The poem imagines an obstacle, which intervenes and, apparently miraculously, guards the man who seemed so helpless from his destroyer.

A Pretty Woman (Vol. VI.) recalls two lines in *Fra Lippo Lippi*—

> "If you get simple beauty and nought else,
> You get about the best thing God invents."

The pretty woman is soulless and cannot love. Why blame her? Rather praise and like—love being beside the mark—the perfection she possesses, prettiness.

"*Childe Roland to the Dark Tower came*" (Vol. V.) is a dream-like, though profoundly connected and coherent, romance. Beyond its demanding some final effort which has cost many lives, the object of Childe Roland's life-long faithful allegiance and pursuit is shrouded in mystery. The atmosphere is one of gloomy horror, heightened by Childe Roland's imagination that every thing about him is set there to do him evil. Nothing appears but he transforms it into something infinitely worse. Sooner than he expects, he comes upon the object of his quest. The conclusion of the poem is tantalising, imagination having been set rocking with expectation of some crowning struggle. We only guess success within the Dark Tower by the fact that Childe Roland lives to tell his tale.

Respectability (Vol. VI.) is a man's congratulation to himself and the woman he loves, either that their union has not received the world's shallow approval, or that they have even temporarily eluded society's conventionalities. The situation is open to either interpretation.

A Light Woman (Vol. V.) is the story of a man who sought a right end by wrong means. He gets himself and the two other persons concerned into a difficult, and, as Browning adds, a particularly dramatic position.

The Statue and the Bust (Vol. V.) is founded on a Florentine legend. In the poem, supineness and irresolution debar the lovers from their paradise, and, though it was, as he says, a sinful one, Browning makes the story serve him for denouncing those faults which are, from his characteristic standpoint, 'sins.'

Love in a Life (Vol. VI.) describes a lover's undaunted chase after the adored one, and her equally constant elusion of his pursuit.

Life in a Love (Vol. VI.) describes the temper which animates the chase of *Love in a Life*. She, the idealised woman, has but to glance back towards her pursuer, and, recovering from failure, he determines to renew the pursuit, though it last his life.

How it strikes a Contemporary (Vol. IV.) tells, in a specified instance, how mistaken a view may be taken of a man by those among whom he lives. The 'poet' is considered to be the King's spy, because of his observant ways. The last paragraph, describing the 'Corrector's' death-bed, gives the man's true status and character.

The Last Ride Together (Vol. V.) shows how musical Browning can make a lyric, which is also a psychological study. A lover can accept his fate, which is parting from his mistress, and in this last ride gather up the rapture of a life-time, since all fail of compassing their own desire, and since the bliss of life spent with his mistress would leave no further heaven to be hoped for. Again, the ride itself may lengthen out into eternity. (Cp. the first half of Stanza x. with *Porphyria's Lover*.)

The Patriot—An Old Story (Vol. V.) tells how the mob treats one who, a year ago, was its darling and saviour.

Master Hugues of Saxe-Gotha (Vol. VI.) represents an organist who desires to summon a dead composer into the organ-loft to tell what his fugues meant. The jangle of a fugue is described, but what vexes the organist is that the business and strife of it all tend to no result. It is therefore, as a form of art, either a discouraging criticism of life, or a false one. The organist decides that it is the latter.

Bishop Blougram's Apology (Vol. IV.) is the first of those 'special pleadings' which are so associated with Browning's name. It is an elaborate piece of casuistry, throughout which we must bear in mind that the Roman Catholic Bishop is talking down an inferior dialectician, rather than seriously arguing. The masterly Blougram is able to make mince-meat of the young, shallow scribbler, Gigadibs, who is, he throughout assumes, really envious of him. Most of the defence, therefore, is ironical, and its fallacies conscious. It represents what a man of Blougram's age and position would be likely to reply to a Gigadibs, when stung to the quick by him. The chief fallacy, which Gigadibs should have immediately questioned, is the comparison of life to the cabin on a six months' voyage. Blougram's putting of comfort before the ideal is directly opposed to the idea of his Church. Blougram's defence is sound when he declares that faith is necessarily struggling; he shows his untruthfulness in averring that this attitude must be masked from others in order to rule them. Blougram is not the gross, cynical worldling he seems. He betrays himself in his reference to Luther. Again, when Gigadibs finally urges the all-importance of truth in one's life (p. 270), Blougram has no argument but to turn the tables and retaliate. At all events, his talk and his counter-criticism of his critic, if they did himself no good, caused a ferment in Gigadibs' mind that led to his relinquishment of merely notional theories. The beauty of many parts of the 'Apology' and the power of all need no pointing out. It is a poem that quickens the intellect at a hundred points.

Memorabilia (Vol. VI.) is supposed to be addressed to some one who had met Shelley but was unmoved by the recollection. To Browning, the fact of the man's having seen Shelley is his one point of interest, the 'eagle-feather' off a blank moor.

Andrea del Sarto (Vol. IV.) was written and sent to a friend in default (!) of a copy of the Pitti portrait called Andrea and his wife. The poem is a study in low tones, its key set by the line—

"A common greyness silvers everything."

Beautiful and interesting as a study, it is not comparable with the poems in which Browning speaks right out from his own heart about his own feelings. Andrea attributes his uninspired life to Lucrezia and to God's 'fetter.' He has sunk into effortless fatalism and doting worship of Lucrezia's beauty. He inertly regrets his misappropriation of Francis the First's money, with no thought of atoning for that fatal dishonesty beyond imagining a certain expiation in resignation to its consequences. We know Lucrezia's stupid, sordid mind through Andrea's talk. It is part of Browning's superb art to characterise a monologue's listener only less clearly than its speaker.

Before (Vol. VI.) gives an onlooker's reasoned assent to a certain duel. One of the fighters (which, is unknown) has been too terribly wronged to make existence possible without this appeal to God. Should the guilty man survive, life may be trusted to punish him. *After* (Vol. VI.) is the survivor's speech. Though victory is with the right, every thing seems unimportant and bearable now, save the terrible fact that the man before him lies slain by his hand.

In Three Days (Vol. VI.) represents a lover's delight in the prospect of rejoining his mistress. He could brave any augury of evil, save that the meeting was to be delayed.

In a Year (Vol. VI.) is the comment of a woman, beautiful, rich, and devoted, on the passing away of her husband's love. She would have done any thing to avert it, and cannot guess the cause. Unconsciously she touches it, and, by the words she imagines the man uttering, we realise his shallow insensibility.

Old Pictures in Florence (Vol. VI.) is a personal utterance, containing the gist of Browning's art philosophy, viz., that aim should transcend accomplishment. The poem's most valuable passage explains wherein early Italian art, imperfect and faulty as it was, marked an advance on the period of Greek sculpture. It is interesting, beside Browning's playful lines, to study Vasari's accounts of the painters cited. The brilliant whimsicalness of the rhymes is in keeping with the serio-comic tone of the piece. 'Carlino' is Carlo Dolci. Stanzas xxi. and xxii. are alien from the ruling idea of the poem and from Browning's general philosophy.[1] They need to be taken dramatically, or as expressing a passing mood in which rest seems the chief good.

In a Balcony (Vol. VII.) is a condensed drama of three characters. The oldish Queen, who, beneath a long frozen exterior is so passionately desirous of love, and Norbert, Constance's lover, who performs his startled part between the two women with veracity and uprightness, are not hard to understand. Constance, whose wits are so subtle, but whose judgment errs into leading herself, Norbert, and the Queen

[1] Contrast *Aristophanes' Apology*, XIII. 8, bottom of page.

into a terrible quandary, is a more complex character. She is a typical woman in her unstraightforward, timorous way of seeking her heart's desire, and in the rapid rising to an occasion wherein she utterly abnegates herself. In playing her mock part before Norbert and the Queen, she is apparently treacherous to love, and we can sympathise with the man's upbraiding of her, but she is really surpassing his imagination of unselfish generosity. Her motive is pure and devoted throughout. The tragic blissfulness of her last sentences convinces us how tenderly she loved Norbert through all her divagation. Her apparent giving of him to the Queen was the effect of a rush of pity and of sympathy with that starved, unfriended heart. She would at all costs spare the cruelty of undeceiving it. She saw, too, how entirely it lay with the Queen to complete or ruin Norbert's cherished career. She partly trusts to his ambition of the greatness she ardently desires for him to make him return the Queen's love, and corroborate the impression made by the ill-advised introduction to the appeal to her for her kinswoman's hand. Constance shows worst in expecting Norbert, at her bidding, to set her aside. She is hurried and excited by the Queen's appearance in a terribly unprepared for juncture, and, ardent with self-denial, hardly realises Norbert's outlook. With time to reflect, she could never have wronged him by believing him capable of the sudden exchange. Neither could she have so blotted out her past with him as to imagine that he takes her seriously, when she pretends, before the stricken Queen, that the interrupted scene was a comedy, and herself all along a smoother of his path to another woman. Norbert fancies the Queen is testing his love for Constance. That Constance herself could propose the test, even as a test, wounds and affronts him. Before his indignation, his unswerving love, her artifice of self-sacrifice breaks down. Norbert and Constance once again know each other and the interrupted perfectness of their love. But that has crossed their lives which cannot be gainsaid—the force of circumstances, and they know that the outraged Queen is sending them the summons of death. *In a Balcony* is a tragedy of circumstances rather than of character.

"*De Gustibus*——" (Vol. VI.) describes an English lane, a tree-loving friend's favourite place, after which Browning accounts for his own taste, in two enchanting sketches of Italy, 'his Italy.'

Women and Roses (Vol. VI.) is a dreamer's tantalising vision of an entrancing rose-tree, bearing three symbolic roses. Round the first rose the beautiful women of the past dance or float; round the second, beautiful living women; round the third, 'beauties yet unborn.' The dreamer appeals to each in turn, but, heedless of him, they only go on each circling their rose.

Protus (Vol. V.) instances how the first may be last, or rather that to be born with a gold spoon in one's mouth is less conducive to empery than to possess an iron will.

Holy-Cross Day (Vol. V.), first of a small group of Jewish poems, realises, from the inside, one of the persecutions Jews bore at 'Christian' hands. Browning penetrates into the upholding Jewish consciousness of being reserved for greater things. The idea in the prayer to Christ is pure Browning and nineteenth century, and would not represent a twelfth century Hebrew, however large-minded.

The Guardian-Angel (Vol. VI.) is one of the rare poems in which Browning lets his love and life look through. Note the beautiful name, 'bird of God,' for an angel, and the inspiring words that conclude Stanza v.

Cleon (Vol. IV.) is another Epistle, comparable with 'the Arab physician's' in that it also touches on the doctrine of Christianity—this time as affecting a contemporary Greek mind. In *Cleon*, however, the problem of life is rather stated than the solution proposed, though such a solution is implicitly associated with the teaching of 'Christus.' The main theme of the poem is the vacuum and disappointment that exist where high culture is nevertheless ignorant of what passes knowledge. The blank wall of death and future non-existence limits the joy of one whose capability for joy has grown infinite. The irony of the merely second-hand life led by the artist, an idea already expressed in *The Last Ride Together* and *In a Balcony* (VII. 31) is expanded here. As in the other epistle, the essence lies in the postscript.

The Twins (Vol. V.) is a parable from Luther,

whose terse vigour of thought and word strikes a responsive chord from Browning.

Popularity (Vol. VI.) is an imaginary utterance suitable to one who appreciated Keats's genius while Keats was living unrecognised. Just as the first fisher of the murex that contained the famous Tyrian purple is unknown and unrewarded, so it is with a new and original poet.

The Heretic's Tragedy (Vol. V.) is a wonderful, quaint account of a horrible 'Act of faith.'

Two in the Campagna (Vol. VI.) opens with a description of the billowy country round Rome, with its pale verdure. The speaker expresses how he and the girl with him experience a moment of mutual supreme emotion, when immediately the thrill is dissipated by some shadow, incomprehension, cooling, that the next moment inevitably brings.

A Grammarian's Funeral (Vol. V.) clothes in a curious and interesting dress Browning's favourite tenet, which may be defined in the words of the Talmud, "It is not incumbent on thee to complete the work: but thou must not therefore cease from it." This lesson the grammarian enforces. His triumphant trust in the endlessness of life saved him from being the mere pedant and layer of an atom of mosaic in erudition's perishable floor. As the corpse bearers wind up the mountain, we seem to feel the cooler air and to hear their heartening chorus.

One Way of Love (Vol. VI.) represents an unselfish

INTRODUCTIONS TO THE POEMS.

lover who has staked his all to win 'Pauline.' He may fail, he knows, perhaps he has already failed, but, if so, he will utter no reproachful nor repining words, but feelingly felicitate another man who succeeds. *Another Way of Love* (Vol. VI.) is a girl's warning speech, in semi-allegoric form, to a 'spoilt' lover. She depicts a selfish man carelessly asking his betrothed if she would 'greatly care' if their engagement were broken off. For reply, she dismisses him with novel asperity, remarking that she is able to live without him, and perhaps choose a better lover, or, should this 'spider' try to weave his web round her again, be careful to speedily demolish it.

"*Transcendentalism. A Poem in Twelve Books*" (Vol. IV.) is addressed by an older poet to a beginner who is producing a work the title names. The experienced man's advice is that beauty and emotion should be a poet's care, rather than the bald, tough expression of metaphysical truth, better suited to prose. The poem's last eight lines are peculiarly fine.

Misconceptions (Vol. VI.) contains a touching little story, preceded by its apologue.

One Word More (Vol. IV.) is the most perfect poetic love-token ever laid at the feet of wife or poet. Like all the words Browning addresses to his 'moon of poets,' this 'word' seems spoken amid a sacred hush. The idea of the artist's longing to have a unique art language whereby to address his beloved is exquisitely dwelt on. Well might Browning regard this poem as separate from his other work, and so classible with Dante's picture, Rafael's sonnets.

Dramatis Personæ, 1864 (Vol. VII.), Browning's next volume, was published after a nine years' interval. We trace in it the deeper thoughtfulness and rarer flashes of ardent fancy that distinguish the bulk of his later from his earlier work. The contents are as follows . . .

James Lee's Wife (originally called *James Lee*) is a wife's chronicle of her husband's estrangement. Mrs. Lee is a similarly charactered wife to those in *A Woman's Last Word*, *Any Wife to any Husband*, *In a Year*, and *Fifine at the Fair*. She is a good, highly strung, but morbid and worrying woman, married to a man of shallow soul, whom she loves deeply. Finding him tired of her, bored by her womanly demands for responsiveness, and probably ruffled by her clear-sighted discernment of his shortcomings, she judges it necessary to his happiness for her to leave him. To her, the companionship of marriage means all or nothing. The poem's nine sections record mood, not action. In I., the wife first detects and dreads the change she dares hardly face. In II., she charges her husband with it. Bitterly, from the depth of her anguished love, she contrasts the apparent warmth and happiness of their life with its inner unsoundness. III. records a deepening of her shuddering sense of change, with a determination to live it down silently. IV. gives the secret of her failure to retain her husband's fancy.

V. is her own noble conception of love, one which, we feel, would be meaningless and irritating to a James Lee. In VI., she criticises a young poet's untested idea of pain. She moans over the pathos of loss and change and the limitation of all achievement, though she can imagine their value. VII. records, by a similitude which the rocks inspire, her resolution to sink all thought of herself in seeking the best course for her husband. VIII. A coarse real hand, beside a beautiful cast from a hand, tells her that duty and labour can survive and transcend the happiness of being loved. In IX., doubt and indecision over, she is leaving James Lee, grievingly, as regards her own feelings, but in the belief that her presence was only an incumbrance and obstacle to his happiness. Her love remains more yearning than ever.

Gold Hair illustrates Browning's love of an eccentricity, a love thinly veiled, in the case of this unpleasing story, under an assumed moralising intention.

The Worst of It is the speech of a man whose wife has deceived and deserted him. His only feeling is self-blame, and intense, pitying regret for her. He wishes he had sinned in her stead, if that might have saved her from her sin and its consequences. He believes God must forgive her, as he does. He would gladly efface himself to efface the silent accusation he knows he is. She has now turned his good to evil, but this evil he regards as self-originating, and his own life as consequently more blamable than hers. 'The worst of it' is that he can do nothing for her who formerly gave him all. He implores her to be good, though not for his sake.

Dîs Aliter Visum represents a woman who recalls to a man the occasion, ten years ago, when he almost proposed to her. She describes the sea-side walk and the man's one moment of sincerity to his ennobling impulse, followed by considerations—of incompatibilities, his age and her youth, and fears of future reproaches and disgust. The considerations choked the impulse, and life's inestimable opportunity was rejected. Two lives, nay, four, have been spoiled. The man measured earthly congruity only, but, in the words of the title, 'it seemed otherwise to the gods.'

Too Late is a man's lament over a dead woman. He never declared his love, and she became the wife of a pitiful rhymer. It was comparatively easy to do without her while she lived. Now she is dead, he feels entirely desolate, and blames himself for his earlier silence. He seeks a shadowy solace from fancying her alive and entirely his, since she is no longer another's.

Abt Vogler is a glorious ascent on the wings of music into a triumphant expression of faith in immortal personality and in heaven's compensation and completion. Abbé Vogler begins with sorrow that his beautiful improvisation is gone, but this is succeeded by the thought that nothing good is ever lost. Through that he rises to the conviction that earth's imperfect will be eternity's perfect. Browning's works hardly contain such another piece of simple perfectness as the definition of a common chord in Stanza vii.

Rabbi Ben Ezra is a poem in which the thinker is subordinated to the thought. It is consequently personal rather than dramatic, and represents Browning's Theism, though not, of course, his Christianity, through an imaginary utterance of the great Rabbi. The leading ideas are (1) The value of age in that it consummates life, and is a peak whence youth may be reviewed, understood, and harmonised. (2) The uses of strife and trial in that they attest our higher nature and our kinship with the Father of spirits. (3) The absolute solitariness of each soul in relation to God, and its independence of earthly estimates. Allied with this is the enduringness of the soul amid the perpetual flux of circumstances. Man must take his means from the Present, but his aim (man being figured by a 'cup'), is solely to slake God's thirst.

A Death in the Desert is the imaginary last scene in the life of the disciple whom Jesus loved. The poem's fictitious setting (the 'parchment' 'supposed of Pamphylax') is exquisitely faithful in its artless simplicity of word and circumstance. Reflecting that with his death the last witness to Christ's life passes away, the dying John recalls his labours and success in making men believe. Death's inspiration upon him, he foresees down the centuries a more fundamental disbelief than his life-time has known. His last word shall be a refutation of disbelief to come. This disbelief will be two-headed, disbelief in Christ being other than a projection from man's mind—(doubt of the Love), and disbelief in a Divine governance associated with miracles, in view of the early superstitions of 'will' everywhere resolved into 'law'—(doubt of the Power). To these doubts John prophetically replies that . . . 'Miracles' guided the child, they are not to coerce the man. Because man knows love and will in himself, and must feel that the acknowledgment of a Divine Love and Power solves earth's problem as nothing else does, he is preferring death to life if he rejects the solution. In reply to the objection against partial truth, imperfect revelation, John urges that only such truth and revelation give men a chance of progressing through the very struggle to obtain better. God gives a gleam, that men may do their part, which is to grow into fuller light through working their own way to it. Browning, through John, accepts this age's doubt as a test and stimulus to faith.

Caliban upon Setebos is one of the most truly creative of Browning's works. Imagining the rudimentary religion of Shakspere's most poor credulous monster, it is in extraordinary contrast with the preceding poem and with Browning's general transcendentalism. It accords with the scientific and strictly natural explanation of the evolution of religion. Caliban's 'moral sense' is the check of fear. He credits Setebos with his own purposeless malignity, sullen jealousy, and cunning, these being his rudimentary idea of Will. Caliban evidences the dualism of primitive belief in his notion of a certain 'Quiet' above Setebos, this being his rudimentary idea of Law. The germ of rites and sacrifices lives in Caliban, the idea of Love is entirely latent. Browning makes his uncouth creature speak of himself in the third person, to suggest his undeveloped sense of personality. This *de*characterisation is not the least brilliant stroke of the poem.

Confessions is a perfect piece of the art of realism, distilling from every-day things a tragic comedy of life.

May and Death has the true touch of nature, recognisable by every one who knows the poignancy of some sight, scent, or sound that is associated with the memory of the dead.

Deaf and Dumb (not included till 1868) was written for Woolner's sculptured group of Sir Thomas Fairbairn's deaf and dumb children. Subject and statues suggested an idea germane to Browning's general conviction that all life's hindrances and limitations contain compensatory blessings.

Prospice is a brave soul's greeting to the enemy, death. With unbandaged eyes, the strong man will essay the last conflict, mindful of its dreadfulness, yet confident in the faith that arms him against fear.

Eurydice to Orpheus (not included till 1868) is an expression of overmastering love. The lines appeared in the Academy Catalogue, 1864, to describe the face of Eurydice, in Sir Frederick Leighton's picture.

Youth and Art is a lighter variation of the theme of *Cristina* and *Dis Aliter Visum*. Two people missed love, once, and once only, within their reach, and, missing love, they miss the best in life.

A Face records a wish to have a certain 'little head' painted in the style most advantageous to its beauty.

A Likeness dwells on the instinct to keep certain associations secret and sacred, and the feeling, half delight, half irritation, when one's heart's hidden treasure is noticed and admired by others. *Marc Antonio* (Raimondi) was the first famous Italian engraver (sixteenth century). Giovanni *Volpato* was Bartolozzi's great pupil (1733-1802).

Mr. Sludge, "The Medium," is, with the exception of *Count Guido Franceschini*, the only one of Browning's special pleadings which is almost undiluted falsehood. The 'medium,' found cheating and brought to bay, gives his own account of the rise and progress of his 'medium'-ship. That his life has been a tissue of the most unwholesome fraud is beyond argument, so he endeavours to throw its odium on his 'patrons,' who may indeed be considered half responsible for the garbage of his soul. They encouraged him from point to point of rappings and manifestations till the production of them became skilled labour. They egged him on to emulate the 'Pennsylvanian mediums.' They petted him for each deeper dip in the morass. They accounted for every ignorance and improbability of the spirits. Sludge loathsomely insinuates that he has at all events been helpful to the cause of religion against atheists. The whole of the 'apology' is eaten through and through with the despicable artifices of luxuriant moral disease, cowardice, and untruthfulness. In the second part, Sludge plausibly expresses his 'belief' in the connection between this world and the supernatural, in divine intervention in so-called 'small' events, and in the selection of certain persons (so why not Sludge?) to gather and interpret such communications. The unmasked character of Sludge only looks through when, Mr. Hiram H. Horsfall leaving him, he is free to indulge in vituperation, and to compose the story whereby he intends to explain their dissolution of amity.

Apparent Failure gives the reflections raised in Browning's mind by the sight of three corpses in the Morgue, and expresses a noble trust in the compassion—and the justice—of God (cp. *In Memoriam* liv.)

Epilogue represents three religious phases: the jubilant worship of David, the bereaved desolateness of Renan, and lastly, a renewed faith, dispensing with symbolism, which Browning declares as his own.

The Ring and the Book, 1868-69, Browning's masterpiece, is one of the longest poems of the century and deals with more life, action, and character than any other. It consists of twelve monologues on one subject, Count Guido Franceschini's murder-case. The first book and the closing one are Browning's prologue and winding up of his huge epic drama. The other ten retrospective monologues are spoken by characters themselves, nine in all, for Count Guido, the defendant, speaks twice, once before his condemnation, once after. Each character recounts the case throughout, and any one monologue, read alone, would, in a sense, give the complete story. So many tellings, and yet no two are alike, and there is no sameness. Each new version gives facts unnoticed by the others, every observation and inference being always exquisitely characteristic of its speaker. *The Ring and the Book* is most free from what Guido calls

'Artistry's haunting curse, the Incomplete.

We feel that Browning has said all that was sayable concerning the celebrated cause which was the talk of Rome early in 1698, and looked at it from the standpoint of all manner of men. Notwithstanding the ring-like clasp of the one poetic imagination, we feel as if we could not be reading one man's work, but as if a magic mirror had been flashed upon the individual mind of each long dead speaker. We are chiefly conscious of this feeling some time after reading the poem, when the recognisable accent of Browning has partially faded, and the mental conceptions remain all the stronger. For us, those obscure Italian people live with more vividness than real, historical characters. The most unskilful reader finds it easy to pick out the defects of a poem written on such a plan as *The Ring and the Book*. A story which is practically known by the end of Book I., and yet is going to be retold again and again, certainly offers no stimulus to curiosity. To Browning, the story as story is nothing, the characters, the souls in strife, are all. How the souls strive, how fail, how conquer, is the matter of real moment. And yet, the circumstances of outer life are rendered pricelessly significant by the soul's taking them for stumbling-blocks or stepping-stones. But that this view of Browning's also applies to his subject-matter, the selection of the Franceschini Trial for a poem in twelve books might be considered capricious. If the main motive is unheroic, and only horrible, out of the meanness, out of the horror, the transcendent virtue of two characters was disciplined into energy of life. Of the dramatic monologues, which cover a space of seven weeks, Guido's are the most uniquely creative. Shakspere has his Iago, Browning his Guido. Guido's presentment, if without comment and entirely self-spoken, would remain absolutely ethical. Throughout his plausible first plea, we want no light other than his own words afford to make us recognise the evil man. The contrast between his two speeches is as marvellous as nature. The most poetic monologues, and, besides Guido's, the only vital ones, are Pompilia's, Caponsacchi's, and the Pope's. The other monologues are spoken by persons less profoundly interested in the Trial, observers, or only secondary actors. Three of them record the world's rumour, outcry, and opinions. They are dim-sighted or indifferent, and frivolously prejudiced. The others are the fustian pleadings of two low-minded lawyers employed on the case. The story from real life two centuries ago which Browning reanimates in *The Ring and the Book* is, free from colouring and briefly, this . . . Pietro and Violante Comparini, an elderly, childless couple, lived in Rome, They loved good living and were well-to-do, but the chief of their property was tied up to pass to some legal heir. Pietro often lamented their childlessness, which rendered them unable to draw on the capital, in the reversion of which they had no personal interest. In 1679 or '80, Violante decided to bargain with a woman of the worst class for her expected infant, and to palm it on Pietro and the world as her own. When in due time the baby girl came, it gladdened Pietro's old heart, and he used to spend his days playing with it. This child afterwards became the heroine and victim of the whole affair, Pompilia. She grew up as unconscious that the Comparini were not her parents as Pietro was that she was not their child. When she was thirteen, Count Guido Franceschini, a nobleman, aged forty-six, needy and fortune-hunting, opened communications with the Comparini through his brother, Abate Paolo, with a view to wedding Pompilia, for her dowry and expectations. The Franceschini allured Violante with visions of their grandeur and greatness, for both of which she was greedy for Pompilia. Pietro, however, on looking into these promises and finding their delusiveness, refused his consent to the match. Thereupon, the unscrupulous and foolish Violante married Pompilia secretly to Guido. Three weeks later, Guido claimed bride and wealth, and the Comparini accompanied Pompilia to live in Guido's palace at Arezzo, stripping themselves of their money in favour of her husband. For four months they endured the penuriousness and savagery of Guido and his relations. Then they fled back to Rome, leaving Pompilia to bear the full brunt. Back in Rome, Violante closed with the Jubilee Indulgence of Innocent XII., to confess her old fraud. Next, the Comparini legally demanded from Guido Pompilia's dowry, and the interest and reversion of the usufruct, on the ground that Pompilia was not their child. The Roman court, in its laodicean way, acknowledged Pompilia's base birth, but decreed the dowry, though not the rest of the estate, to Guido. Now began Pompilia's tragedy in her husband's rage and hate levelled against her. A letter, purporting to be from her, but really traced in ink, over her husband's pencilling, by Pompilia, who could neither read nor write and was ignorant of its contents, was received in Rome by Abate Paolo. It represented Pietro and Violante in the worst light, and accused them of giving Pompilia a parting injunction to find some gallant in whose company she could follow them as soon as possible, previously pillaging and burning her husband's house and poisoning its inmates. The document was not only used as a return weapon against the Comparinis' outcry against Guido, but was also intended to pave the way for what Guido, with wicked cunning, now set his whole brain to effect. His desire was to get rid of Pompilia without ostensibly driving her away, so that the money might be his. Abetted by his mother and brother, he tormented his patient girl-wife with unremitting cruelty and outrage to body and soul. This continued for three years. Guido did his secret utmost to force her into an intimacy with Giuseppe Caponsacchi, a young Aretine Canon, which should justify him in divorcing her, but she proved incapable of guile. At last, in April 1697, Pompilia knew she was to be a mother, and then the one drear hope left her of losing her life under Guido's cruelty changed into the mother's obligation to preserve her child. She must flee. But how? The Archbishop and Governor of Arezzo and a friar had long ago refused or failed to help her, even when she told them that her miseries tempted her to suicide. Her thoughts turned to the stranger, Caponsacchi, whose name was hourly hissed in her ear, and she spoke to him from her terrace and besought him to help her to escape to those she called her parents. Ennobled by the demand upon him, Caponsacchi gave her such help as an angel might give a saint, and took her towards Rome. The husband, whose longed for chance had come, slyly noted all, and, in discreet time, followed. At Castelnuovo, last stage before Rome, he overtook the fugitive and the priest. Pompilia had perforce halted for a few hours at the inn, so dangerous did she believe her journeying farther without rest would be, after the two days and nights of continuous flight. In that inn, Pompilia, for the first and last time, confronted her husband with flaming wrath, and even attempted to take his sword and kill him. This she did, in irrepressible indignation at Guido's false charge against her innocent deliverer of criminal elopement with her. The very constables, called in by the coward, Guido, felt for the moment the greatness of truth as uttered by Pompilia. It did not suit Guido's purpose to slay then and there (as his partisans afterwards regretted), for that might have lost him Pompilia's money. Avarice as well as cowardice held him back. Instead, he handed Caponsacchi and Pompilia to the Public Force to be conveyed to Rome. Just as he had previously forged letters purporting to be from Pompilia, and had them delivered to Caponsacchi at Arezzo, so now he pretended to pick up in the inn, as left behind by Pompilia and Caponsacchi, a bundle of the most incriminating 'love-letters.' These letters, written by Guido, he hid and found, that they might bear witness against the two. When Guido brought the case before the Court, the ambiguous decision given again showed the half-heartedness, miscalled moderation, of the Roman Tribunal. Caponsacchi was relegated for three years to Civita, and Pompilia was sent to bide cloistered with the Convertites, Guido being virtually deprived of his wife for the time being: The sentence was half-condemnation, half-acquittal, Caponsacchi's relegation being distinctly termed no exile. The Comparini now demanded in Pompilia's name her divorce on the ground of cruelty, which plea Paolo tried to frustrate by demanding on the other side a divorce. Meanwhile, at Arezzo, Guido lay wallowing in rancour and brooding over his townsfolks' mockery. Presently, the Convent was allowed to open its door, and Pompilia passed from one nominal detention to another, this time going to the Comparini. They took her to their villa outside Rome, where, shortly after, her child, Gaetano, was born. Hearing of this, the black blood of Guido surged indeed. It was at last free to surge, for the birth of a child, his heir and Pompilia's, would secure him the money in any case. For days he meditated and arranged his last frightful deed. On the second night of the year 1698, he stole disguised to the villa, with four cutthroats. He entered it, and with countless stabs killed the Comparini and Pompilia, they aged seventy, she seventeen. But Pompilia, though mortally wounded and left for dead, was not to die till she had been able to make the truth apparent. That she might survive long enough for that was her silent prayer as Guido struck. She lived four days, to explain her life, to pardon Guido, and to vindicate and glorify Caponsacchi. Guido killed Pompilia because he had never tempted her into sin, because he never could prove any thing against her, and therefore his cheated avarice, and his pride turned into shame had been so long balked of revenge. Guido's hirelings had already resolved to kill him for non-fulfilment of his promise of payment, but that was intercepted by their being all caught red-handed. The frenzy of his hate had made Guido forget one precaution of flight, viz., to secure the warrant for hiring post-horses. The murderers were found tired out twenty miles from the villa. They were carried to Rome, and, after a month's Trial, were executed, the noble being beheaded, the others hanged. They were first condemned by the civil court, when Guido's advocate, thinking to save him astutely, pleaded the fact of his being in some sort a cleric, and therefore privileged to appeal to the Church. Leniency was expected of the aged Pope, but Innocent, when he had mastered the matter, unhesitatingly sealed the doom of Guido and his ruffians. The execution took place on February 22nd, 1698, in the Piazza del Popolo, where a scaffold, with the framed axe (*mannaia*), was erected, flanked by two gibbets. Public feeling was immensely stirred by the Trial and its conclusion. The more so, that Guido, the husband, the man of position and influence, in whose favour the strange facts of the case could so easily be distorted, had the suffrage of the superficial majority. . . . Such are the broad facts of Pompilia's story, omitting the dramatic picturesqueness of details and minor actions which are the flesh and blood of it.

I. *The Ring and the Book* is the special title of the

opening section In it Browning lays before his readers (1) the meaning of the title, (2) the origin of the poem, (3) glimpses of the story and of the contents of the old book, its foundation, (4) the justification of his imaginative presentation of it, and (5) his invocation to the dead singer, his wife, under the name of 'lyric Love, half angel and half bird.' (1) The notion of the Ring Browning gained from the Roman jewellers, who mix a harder alloy with gold in order to beat and emboss it into a ring with carved devices. The ring finished, the alloy is easily detached. So Browning intends to mix the gold of fact with the 'alloy' of fancy, without which it could never be forged and filed into shape. This 'fancy,' moreover, what is it but a higher 'fact'? (2) He tells how he found the Book, the small-quarto that contained the contemporary records of the Franceschini Trial, how he fused its facts with his own insight and realisation, the Book with the 'Ring,' and how, months after, in London, he knew the time had come for writing what his spirit had been chafing to life. (3) Browning recounts his first glowing imagination of the story as its successive scenes flashed upon his mental retina on that June night on his terrace in Florence. This first telling of the tale, fragmentary as it is, strikes the keynote of the truth at once, by giving Browning's own view of the characters and their action. Portions of the old book, facts and comments taken from it, are previously given. These are deeply interesting in their place and chiefly as showing the comparative deadness of the Book without the metal that helps to make the Ring. (4) Then comes a superb imaginative account of how such a work as *The Ring and the Book* comes into existence, how a man's living spirit breathes, Elisha-like, upon the seeming corpses and informs them with his own abounding life. Browning next gives the condition, inside and outside, of all his speakers at the time of their speaking. The passages descriptive of the two Halves of Rome, *Tertium Quid*, Count Guido Franceschini, Caponsacchi, Pompilia, Dom. Hyacinthus de Archangelis, Giovambattista Bottinius, the Pope, and Guido are each prefatory to its proper monologue. Browning explains his reason for presenting the one series of actions from so many stand-points. He wished to be faithful to the sincerity and reach of real life, and also to show how warped and how cruel is a narrow, slothful, or selfish estimate of whatever partakes of life's baffling obscurations and changes. (Note on p. 55 the magical touches whereby Browning impersonates Winter and Summer.) (5) In the lovely posy of his Ring, Browning speaks first of his lyric Love's ante-earthly existence, and of her life on earth. Then, in an exalted strain mingled with pleading, he speaks of her as retranslated to and gladdening heaven, and yet accessible to his word that invokes her blessing on every work begun and ended by him.

II. *Half-Rome* is the name of the first dramatic monologue, the drift of which is

"How Half-Rome found for Guido much excuse."

The speaker is a man predisposed to side with Count Guido from the fact that he is himself a suspicious husband. He is just leaving San Lorenzo, the Comparinis' parish church, where Pompilia, who is now dying in the hospital, was baptized and married. There, on this, the day following the murder, Pietro and Violante's bodies are laid out for public inspection, at their feet the notched dagger that dealt the fatal wounds. As this sample of Half-Rome leaves the church, where, with the rest of the crowd, he has been gloating over the horrible spectacle, he meets an acquaintance. This person is promptly button-holed, and has the benefit of hearing the story of the Franceschini Case, as rumour has filtered it in and bias filtered it out again of the head piece of the worthy who addresses him. 'Half-Rome' takes it for granted that the deposition that is expected from Pompilia in the hospital is the confession of her crime. He considers the case extremely simple, in fact only open to one construction, which is, guilt on Pompilia's part, rank roguery on the Comparinis', and on Guido's, justifiable reprisals, unwisely deferred, it is true. Throughout the account, Guido's avarice plays no part. In describing the match-making between Violante and the Franceschini, 'Half-Rome' only sees Violante's blind greed of grandeeship. Guido is supposed solely to care for a fair young wife to brighten up his dingy palace.

The speaker unquestioningly accepts Guido's report that he and his household were drugged and his escritoire rifled by Pompilia when she fled. Having no particular standard of goodness and integrity, he considers nothing so likely as cowardice and deceit. The dutiful and pure Pompilia, and the soldier-priest, her champion, are as entirely beyond his range as beings of a different sphere. Yet even 'Half-Rome's' words cannot conceal the potency of truth in their speech and action when Guido came upon them in the inn. The revelation is nevertheless unrecognised by the speaker's own dull soul. 'Half-Rome' fancies that he allows facts to speak for themselves, and every now and then reiterates how unprejudiced his statement is. It is only by comparing the monologue with others, that we appreciate the fine touches of descriptive phrase whereby Browning discloses the bent of the speaker.

III. 'The Other Half-Rome,' addressing his audience two days later, finds the wife innocent. His speech is coloured by the thought of Pompilia as she lies in the hospital, surrounded by gazers. Like all who have seen her, the speaker is touched by the pitifulness of her youth. From no merit of his own, but because he has half fortuitously espoused Pompilia's side, and because his discourse opens with a sympathetic description of her dying hours, his account of the case comes nearer truth than 'Half-Rome's.' 'The Other Half-Rome' laments Violante's falsification of Pompilia's parentage, but says all he can in favour of the arrangement. He stigmatises the Comparinis' inconsiderate foolishness in apprising Guido of his wife's base birth. They might have known that Guido would deny their story and never give up Pompilia as long as he had the remotest chance of gaining money through her. Nevertheless, like the former sample speaker, this one is inclined to give a choice of readings of the events, and, like the Court, ruminate both, instead of rejecting one and nourishing himself on the other. A wonderful touch—puzzling to the speaker—of Pompilia's purity comes out in this narration, in the inconsistency between her story and Caponsacchi's (both told the Court eight months earlier) as to whether it was evening or day-break when they reached Castelnuovo. In the confusion of utter exhaustion, Pompilia believed that it was morning when they entered the inn. 'The Other Half-Rome' is keenly aware of Guido's main motive, his prompter and check, avarice. Though he registers Pompilia's innocence, the insult done to God in her murder is not what strikes him. Rather, as a law-abiding citizen, speaking in the interests of all, he condemns Guido for supplementing and correcting a decision previously pronounced by law. The Molinists are continually in and out of the discourses, any thing and every thing being attributed or compared to their heresy. Such references secure the approval of every orthodox listener, and agreeably attest the speaker's soundness. The lesson Browning enforces by these specimens of 'human estimation,' the two Halves of Rome, he impresses by the curious variety in their statement of events, and the differing motives they assign to an action. Compare the two presentments of Violante's motive in her Jubilee confession, the two accounts of Pompilia's flight from Guido's house, and the two explanations of Guido's pass-word at the villa door.

IV. *Tertium Quid* views the trial from an angle different from either of the foregoing. He is the veritable *tertium quid* of chemistry, the neutral salt. Despising the vulgar partisanship of street and market-place, this dispassionate third party holds a middle course. His particular listeners are an Excellency and a Highness, grouped in an embrasure of a fashionable saloon. *Tertium Quid* might reasonably be expected to allow for an instinctive bias in favour of a nobleman, but he is far too judicial to let this interfere with his full recognition of the evidence against Guido. He opens with a masterly sketch of aristocratic poverty, and shows a general disposition to adorn the tale and omit its less effective points. He supplies characteristic new details, such as the first introduction of Pompilia's name to the Franceschini by the 'woman-dealer in perukes.' With his show of fairness, he leaves the case exactly where he found it, taking back anything he has said that may seem to lean to either side. He appears to consider the refusals of the Aretine authorities to respond to her appeals a strong point against Pompilia, and then goes on to reprehend her for escaping under the escort of a fashionable young priest. He sneers at Caponsacchi's ready acceptance of Pompilia's woeful story. *Tertium Quid's* stupidity is of heart, not brain. He concludes by avowing that the case is extremely turbid, as indeed he has made it appear to himself and others by his cynical summing up of 'six of one and a half a dozen of the other.' Not that he cares. His main object is to stand well with his fastidious audience, and he has catered for its taste accordingly.

V. Count Guido Franceschini now pleads his cause before his judges. He and his associates have been tortured up to the point deemed necessary for ascertaining truth, and have, under torture, confessed to the murder. 'Not guilty' being therefore a plea out of the question, the best Guido can now do for himself is to extenuate the 'irregular deed.' He flatters his judges, strives to enlist their compassion, and addresses himself to their prejudices. He takes his stand on his regard for authority, the Church, and law. Every act of his life has run in a prescribed groove. Younger brothers are free to become soldiers or churchmen, he, an eldest son, was bound to support the house at home, to marry, and continue the Franceschini line. He describes his married life as a torture to pride and self-respect, which no rack even mimics. He poses as a servant of law who would not move in the first instance till law gave the cue. Here, changing his tone to one of simulated indignation, he reproaches the Court for the inadequacy of its previous judgment, which yet he proves to have been so far an implicit condemnation of Pompilia (as to its shame, it was) as to justify her husband and victim in supplementing it with nature's justice. Thus he lays the burden of proof on the Judges themselves. He skilfully works up to the birth of the child as the climax of his maddening grievance. With the utmost nimbleness in fence, he perpetually shifts his ground, as in his alternative hypothesis regarding the child's parentage, so as to make it serve his purpose equally well either way. Guido professes the innocence which can afford to bring its secret things to light. Of course he makes the most of every thing that can by any possibility tell in his favour, making nothing, or a distortion, of what tells against him. Like *Tertium Quid*, he frankly acknowledges the marriage a barter, and, on his side, a fair bargain. He does not deny that he wrote the letter which Pompilia traced over, because it is a husband's duty to guide, and, if need be, coerce his wife into the right path. He makes light of his cruelties to Pompilia as harshness excusable to his disappointment in her, and warranted by her levity. After all, they were threatenings and frightenings rather than actual penalties, and her elopement proved their inefficacy. Every trifle in the speech is significant, and not only the conscious, but the unconscious touches, as where Guido, in describing his wish to get back to Vittiano from Rome, mentions as Vittiano's attraction that "one limes flocks of thrushes there." The fiend of guile consummates his hypocrisy in the description he gives of his enlisting the sympathies of his four assistants (no 'bravo-hiring'), and of his waiting through the Christmas season, its 'Good will to man' battling against the call of his dread duty. His infamous use of Caponsacchi's name at the villa door that night he twists into the last supreme chance given by him to Pompilia. That failing, he pretends he would have even then spared the slaughter, had not his arch-enemy, Violante, appeared first at the door.

VI. Giuseppe Caponsacchi's is the first certainty among the dramatic monologues, the first which is entirely free from moral confusion. Caponsacchi has been summoned from Civita to retell, in the changed circumstances caused by the murder (of which they have just made him aware), the story he told the same Court after the arrest at Castelnuovo. This time he is called in to give counsel. At once he breaks out into stern condemnation of his judges, whose base torpidness of eight months ago is responsible for the fresh terrible wrong. Awe-struck now, they listen to him, till one weeps, another can no longer keep his place. The whole glorious speech quivers with impassioned wrath, pity, and sorrow. One vision inspires it all, that of the 'snow-white soul,' Pompilia, who 'is only dying while' they speak.

'Sirs,
'Only seventeen!'

Caponsacchi's character from earliest youth had had a prophecy written upon it. He was one whose deeper nature only slumbered till some enthusiasm should evoke it. The day he "was blessed by the revelation" of Pompilia and she made her appeal to him was his spirit's birthday. The grand offer of his life and test of his worth came and he accepted them. All the hollow nothings he had previously lived in were burnt up like withered leaves. He instantly recognised that the real and true and sure were with Pompilia, and threw conventionalities to the winds. Nothing can be more beautiful than the description of how Pompilia and Caponsacchi knew each other instantly by the look, except his account, so serious and so simple, of the journey between Arezzo and Castelnuovo. From first to last, Caponsacchi's feeling for Pompilia, which he is careful to tell his judges is 'not love,' because he recollects their titter of eight months back, is indeed love and religion too. He himself cannot designate it except as "faith, the feeling that there's God." Deep down and unfolded in the characters of Pompilia and Caponsacchi is the human love that exists between a true man and a pure woman when they love each other. This love was in their case crystallised at its first stage, at that absorbed devotion to the beauty of each other's characters, which is really an interchange and elevation of hearts, transfiguring the rest of life into responsibility and thankfulness. Caponsacchi never ceases to wonder at people's dulness of perception, at the cruel blindness of the Court's jog-trot procedure. He himself has been so quick to seize rights and wrongs, so ready to succour and redress, a chivalrous soul with no selfish dross. Heaven and hell are no farther apart than Caponsacchi and Guido, the incarnations of devotion and hate. The worst regret for himself that Caponsacchi has is that he did not extirpate Guido when he might. All the tears and irony of life, as it is mirrored in *The Ring and the Book*, are concentrated in Caponsacchi's last line, which is also in a sense the reaction from the selfless bravery of what precedes it,

'O great, just, good God ! Miserable me !'

That is the bitter cry of a man who rebels from his soul against the misnomers of society, the unutterably pathetic captivity of good to ill, the world's old error of crucifying its divinity.

VII. Pompilia's is the crowning monologue of the cycle. Lying in the lazar-house, with her 'twenty-two wounds, five deadly,' which, as she characteristically words it, the "surgeon cared for her, to count," she is full of gentle gratitude for the least services. So lying and so speaking, Pompilia retraces her years of nightmare and her few months of peace. Because she has lived to know the bliss of seeing her child and had it lying on her breast two days, the peace seems to obliterate the anguish. On the third day, the child was taken away to be safer from its father. But no; Pompilia cannot have that, her boy never had a father, only a mother—and God to leave it with. Pompilia rejoices that Guido himself annulled their marriage by slaying her, saved as by fire the life he had polluted. The name, Gaetano, and the pathetic reason why Pompilia chose it for her boy throw light on what Caponsacchi could not understand in the flight from Arezzo, when her mind was wandering, and he thought she meant 'Caponsacchi' when she murmured 'Gaetano.' Browning represents in Pompilia motherhood idealised and glorified, from that vivid day-break in the preceding April to this her death-day. Pompilia would not be Pompilia if she were entirely to palliate Violante's falsity, the first cause of all the woe. 'It was wrong, or rather mistake, like almost all her life.' The Comparini, her 'poor parents,' as she calls them, meant well by her, and that must be enough. . Even for the malignant Count Guido Pompilia can make some excuse. He was cheated in the first instance, and she, by being innocent and uncomprehending, thwarted and angered him the more. A wonderful touch of the mother's sympathy is in the line,

"I could not love him, but his mother did."

The outside world may think that Caponsacchi failed in his attempt to serve Pompilia, but Pompilia knows otherwise. Caponsacchi effected the turning-point in her miseries, every thing since then has been happiness or at least peace, and the murder, that too has wrought good. Apart from consequences, Caponsacchi's deed and example have been a priceless boon,

> "Through such souls alone
> God stooping shows sufficient of His light
> For us i' the dark to rise by. And I rise."

Pompilia is incomparable for absolute simplicity and naturalness in the story of a short, strange, sorrowful life. We see Pompilia as the pitiable little bride, the victim in the wolf's den, thrown him like a bone to mumble and be kept quiet by, the overtaken and slandered fugitive, and lastly the two weeks' mother hacked to pieces. The submissiveness, the conscience, and the rectitude shine through at every stage of the narrative, and beside them Pompilia's humility, and unconsciousness, as she explains her life, of her own sanctity and loveliness of character.

VIII. Dominus Hyacinthus de Archangelis next speaks. He is the Procurator of the Poor, who is to defend Guido and his four associates. This monologue contains the rough notes of the defence, interspersed with asides. These chiefly refer to the advocate's little boy, his Giacinto, on whose name is lavished every affectionate diminutive of which the Italian language is capable, and in honour of whose eighth birthday a feast is to be held to-night. The doting papa cares very much more about 'old curly-pate' and the preparation of the lamb's fry and other delights, than for the Franceschini Case.

INTRODUCTIONS TO THE POEMS.

The pleading is very humorous, and would be extremely amusing, if the sport of it were not so incongruous with the deadly realities it juggles with. Its life-likeness is perhaps the stronger for the irony. Arcangeli's defence is based on the 'Cause of Honour,' to vindicate which a man may do anything, equally so if the injury be only misprision of the fact. Texts are wrested and preposterous instances alleged to support this. Arcangeli constantly has an eye to the detested Fisc, his adversary, whom he means to rout by Latinity as well as logic. The speech is sprinkled with verbal bows and scrapes to the Judges, and Arcangeli has good hopes that his production will reach the Pope, poor dotard though he be, and even that his treatment of the case will be adopted by him. With professional identification, Arcangeli speaks of Guido as 'we' and 'ourselves,' a humorous touch in its suggestion of the contrast between the comfortable family man and the malevolent hater, his client. The entire argument is, of course, a sham, having nothing to do with the question at issue. If a word shows reluctance at being hitched into the lawyer's Latin, he discards it for a more amenable one, even if it contradicts fact, because if one Judge goes upon law, another considers style. Nothing can be more absurd than the defence of Guido's 'helpmates,' whom the Procurator metamorphoses into equitable, though immature, rustics. At last the string of quibbles is finished, and Arcangeli delightedly thrusts it into a pigeon-hole, feeling his evening's domestic joy honestly earned.

IX. Juris Doctor Johannes-Baptista Bottinius is the public prosecutor, upon whom has devolved the conduct of the proceedings against Guido. This monologue supposes Bottini trying over to an imaginary audience his final speech on the Case. In it, we see how another kaleidoscopic lawyer can shake up the facts and variegate them afresh. Bottini's nominal task is to vindicate Pompilia's fame, but he proposes a harder, *i.e.*, to admit, for argument's sake, every calumnious evidence against her, and yet bring her out triumphing. Accordingly, his oration, which opens with a self-displaying flourish, is as futile, and more offensive, than Arcangeli's. Bottini's waggish quips and abhorrent insinuations are so glaringly unseemly that the whole discourse is a burlesque. 'Peccadillos' are the natural element of Bottini's imagination, and to assume them in Pompilia gives him so much the better chance of exercising a sympathetic ingenuity in explaining her actions, that he meets the objection of her death-bed statements by depreciating them as a 'genial falsehood,' which her (previous) last sacrament absolved. The similitudes with which Bottinius garlands the case aptly mark his bestial nature. To him, 'our paragon,' as he terms Pompilia, was an alluring, rosy daughter of Eve, who may easily be forgiven, nay, applauded, for having escaped womanhood's 'greatest sin, impudence,' though by the exercise of 'feint, wile, and trick,' viz., by enticing an enamoured priest to her aid by meretricious promises, by a process described as 'splendidly mendacious.' The action that the Fiscal most admires throughout the case is clearly Guido's appeal to Law, and what he defends with perhaps his greatest ingenuity is the answer Law then delivered.

X. As soon as we open the Pope's deliberation, we feel, in the weight and fruitfulness of its every word, that it is the conclusion of the whole matter. It seems as though the fragmentary human judgments were cleared away, while the Pope anticipates the divine view of each of the characters concerned in the case, judging the life by the talents. Much was given to Guido, little to Pompilia, thereby making the one so much the more guilty, and the other so much the more admirable. The meditation represents the after-thoughts of the aged Pontiff, who has already inflexibly determined on confirming the legal sentence on Guido and his accomplices. The principal note of the Pope is his sense of responsibility, his conviction that life is a grave, earnest affair, a conflict to the last, its 'business being just the terrible choice' between white and black, any evasion of which choice is grievous sin. Though calm and cheerful as to his judgment, the Pope is oppressed by the immense gravity of the decision, this sending of five souls into eternity just before his own. Precedents of human judgment are unsustaining, the records of the Papacy only chronicling the cobwebs of 'infallibility.' Yet

the Pope is not disconcerted, nor would he be even if
the after-time proved his judgment mistaken, for he
is acting up to his light, and he knows that God
values the intention, or 'seed of act.' The truth he
has evolved painfully from the case, he holds tenaci-
ously, and that is enough for him. The Pope recognises as Pompilia's peculiar grace her brave change
from endurance to resistance at the first whisper of
responsibility. What he chiefly emphasises in the evil
course of Guido is his rejection of each chance of
repentance. Stern as is the condemnation, and rueful
the outlook for Guido's future, the Pope thinks it
possible that his sentence may yet save Guido's soul,
by the very suddenness of retribution. He therefore
speaks of Guido's arrest, which prevented him from
being murdered by his companions, as a mercy-stroke
of respite. Nearly half the Pope's soliloquy has
regard to the ultimate foundations of his judgment.
His responsibility is so grave that it carries his
thoughts to the first principles of his faith. He
acknowledges the doubt urged upon him by the
weakness and guilt of professed Christians, whereas
human nature without Christianity is capable of heroism like that which he has been considering to-day,
and of belief in virtue for virtue's sake, as Euripides
testifies. The Pope meets the trial to belief which
such facts suggest and acknowledges its severity.
Yet he overbears it by the thought (so characteristic
of Browning, when, as in *Rabbi Ben Ezra*, *Ferishtah*,
and here, we listen to his own verifiable tones), that

in the very weakness of a religion is the greatest incentive to love and help it—

> "So, never I miss footing in the maze,
> No,—I have light nor fear the dark at all."

The Pope believes that each age has its peculiar trial, and, through the inertness and depravity of his own time of too assured noonday, he foresees a coming period when 'faith in the report' will be bravely broken, 'through increased faith in the thing reported.' The somewhat fearful and aged tone that his reflections on the future assume, presently changes into a reiteration of his individual determination to witness to the last for Christ—which witness is on this occasion expressed by his sentence on these particular malefactors. Guido's death shall fulfil the two aspects of such punishment, and deter as well as avenge.

XI. Guido next speaks—to the two churchmen who have been sent to prepare him for execution. He is no longer the Count Franceschini, wary in defence, but a raging animal, best described by his own word, 'wolf.' He clings with desperate cowardice to the faint hope of intercession and reprieve, and therefore fawns, as he begins by doing, intermittently, on his appalled friends. The horrible prospect of the severing axe, the near moment when he, so alive now, will be literally cut off from among the living, vibrate all through the mockery and ferocity of his language. The speech is a rift into the hell of Guido's

naked mind. He alternately pleads innocence and
guilt, provocation and irresponsible wolfishness. He
calls the Pope the 'murderous old man' who incon-
sistently pushes a soul into perdition. He accuses
the present Cardinal and Abate, the Pope, and the
whole Christian world of being in a league of hypocrisy,
killing him because he is the one sinner among them
who has been frank. 'He will not pay religion and
morality their toll of confession. Why should he
satisfy their self-interested desire? Repentance will
not save his life. At least, he will tell no lies to
please others. His last words shall be truth. The
social pact defines one man's pleasure as another's
pain. Law, therefore, prohibits undue pleasure.
Guido's life has disregarded this. He now pays for
it.' . . . 'Religion and irreligion are meaningless
and interchangeable terms. Love of life is the unspoken motive of everybody. Guido has recognised
no law he could not see. He has at least been
sincere, not played fast and loose with God like
these hypocrites. Because he has had the courage
of their opinions, the others have felled him in self-
defence.' . . . 'Why, among all the incredibilities
people accept, is his tale of maddened jealousy solely
disbelieved?' . . . 'He could not choose his temperament, his failure was a blunder, not a crime.' Guido
describes his detestation of Pompilia, of the patience,
stillness, and meekness which enraged him beyond
all other causes. Caponsacchi's name hardly occurs,
since to Guido he had no real existence. Guido's

intensest hate of Pompilia is hate of her saintliness and spiritual independence of him. Her eyes haunt him, most unbearable in their 'abnegation of revenge.' 'Pompilia and the old pretentious fools, the Comparinis, formed a Chimæra, kid, lion, and serpent, which he had no peace till he slew.' Guido regards cringing and feigning as the wisdom of the weak, just as plaguing, browbeating, and plundering are the instinct and prerogative of the strong. He loathed Pompilia because she never cringed nor feigned. 'Guido's life has been one long warfare with humanity, and luck has been against him just when he seemed (at the inn, after the murder, on his Trial, with the Pope) touching success.' . . . 'Let him die, life would have nothing to offer.' Once more Guido scathingly satirises his dissimulating, material age, and then plunges frantically into the central abyss of moral darkness. The lurid gloom is almost grand. Guido seems to shed his mean manhood, and become an embodied hate, which may, he suggests, be yet transformed when its uses have been exhausted. . . . 'Guido has raved because he thought they would not slay impenitence.' Now he dashes hither and thither, alternately begging for life and foaming at those who cannot grant it. As his doom begins to close round him in approaching steps and voices, Guido's last shriek gathers up the concentrated essence of the Franceschini case in one word—

"*Pompilia*, will you let them murder me?"

XII. In *The Book and the Ring*, Browning winds up the loose threads that remain. Details of Guido's execution, aftermath of opinions, and the survivors' subsequent dealings, each after his kind, are given. Some of these are contributed as by private correspondents, two of whom, Arcangeli and the Fisc, are familiar to us. Browning veritably found the groundwork of their letters in the old Book. We learn from one that the 'poor Count's' end evinced the decorum and piety of most reported executions. The writers unite in misjudging 'old Somebody,' as the Pope is nicknamed. Bottini encloses in his letter a paragraph from the sermon of Brother Celestine, Pompilia's last confessor. The extract is a comment on the seeming rule of wrong, and the weakness, which, even more than wickedness, falsifies fact. Though the Augustinian's summary of human affairs is apparently mournful, it really belongs to Browning's entire view, implicitly strongest in *The Ring and the Book*, that life is a paradox, and that probation and postponement are the earth's most valid words. Browning's ultimate hopefulness is not clouded by the perplexities of Pompilia's story. It is only tempered to the range and depth of its subject, life, across whose worst welter Browning still detects God's hand, in 'accident' or human service, just, and only just, upholding the earnest believer. As in life itself, there are so many lessons in *The Ring and the Book* that it seems artificial and futile to emphasise one above another. It is enough that Caponsacchi and Pompilia and the Pope rise, while Guido falls. In Browning's wise words—

> "it is the glory and good of Art,
> That Art remains the one way possible
> Of speaking truth,"

because

> "Art may tell a truth
> Obliquely, do the thing shall breed the thought."

Balaustion's Adventure; including a Transscript from Euripides, 1871 (Vol. XI.), is a memorial of that affectionate preference for Euripides, shared by Mr. and Mrs. Browning, and already partly explained in a passage in 'The Pope.' Euripides' humanity and pathos appealed to Mrs. Browning, as the motto of *Balaustion's Adventure*, taken from her *Wine of Cyprus*, indicates, and a congeniality exists between Browning and Euripides as poets, for the last of the three Greek tragedians was, like Browning, not only an innovator and an extender of bound in art, but a poet of 'hard matter and harsh manner,' and a lover of colloquial phrase. The *Transcript* is a translation of that most touching story, the *Alkestis*, interspersed with Browning's explanations of the characters. An ethical exhibition of the subject is thus interwoven with Euripides' dramatic colloquies, while Browning's comments are dramatised in form by being put into the mouth of an imaginary Greek reciter of the play. This is Balaustion, a Rhodian maiden, who introduces her recitation of *Alkestis* by narrating her 'Adventure' to four Athenian friends.

She describes how her love and retention of Euripides' poetry saved her life and the lives of a whole ship's crew the year after the disastrous Syracusan expedition of Nikias. A sudden wind drove the Kaunian ship upon the hostile coast of Sicily, and the Syracusans would have forced it back to be the prey of a pursuing pirate-bark, had not the 'lyric girl' undertaken to save her companions by repeating to the Syracusans the tragedy of *Alkestis*, as she remembered hearing it in the theatre at Kameiros. The verisimilitude of the 'Adventure' is founded on Plutarch's Life of Nikias, where the episode of the saving of a crew by the power of Euripides' poetry is given. The Sicilian Greeks were known to be athirst to hear more of the new poet, and merciful to such of their prisoners as could recite any fragments from him.

In thinking of Browning as a translator of *Alkestis*, we have to think of the modern spirit, with its obstinate questionings, set to work upon the most perplexing of ancient stories. There is a deep problem in the strange correlation of its characters, a problem which Euripides states and does not solve. We have to imagine how the mystery and anguish of *Alkestis* writhed in Browning's mind as he mused on the tale till he felt compelled to probe its significance as well as translate its words. Then, probably, the recollection of Plutarch's sympathetic legend came to him, and in the eager and tender 'Wild-pomegranate-flower' he found an artistic means for his own commentary on Alkestis, Admetos, and Herakles. The story of the self-immolating wife, who consents to die in the place of her cowardly husband, and is rescued from Hades by Herakles in gratitude for the hospitality of Admetos, has been transformed and conformed to conventional ideas by many a modern poet. While their Admetos is divested of definiteness in order to divert attention from his baseness, their Alkestis becomes blindly worshipful of the ignoble husband who lets her die for him. This rose-water Alkestis is a phantasm compared with the intensely real, intensely moving Alkestis of Euripides, who consents to sacrifice herself, but whose love for Admetos freezes in the act, and whose last words, so self-measuring, austere, and joyless, ignore his fluent lamentations, and solely regard the future she may well fear for her children. It would seem as though Euripides, true to his age, neither sought nor cared to seek any solution of the questions that his heart-aching story would call up to a modern writer who attempted to represent so daring a subject. .That ineffable disdain for Admetos, how is it to be forgotten in the restored life of Alkestis? What is the strange irony whereby Herakles wrests Alkestis from Death, not because of his admiration of her heroism, but because Admetos had the courteous self-control to let him feast in his palace while he and his people were mourning? Browning's courageous intellect attempts to bridge the moral chasm between the husband and wife by making

Alkestis the story of the development of a soul in Admetos. Three-fourths of the Balaustion-Browning commentary trace the gradual awakening of Admetos, by means of loneliness and loss, to be a worthier companion of the restored Alkestis. Euripides, indeed, superficially brings this about. But, with him, the repentance of Admetos is little better than an increasing self-pity, a growing sense that what with the taunts of enemies and the widowed halls, his lot is harder than to have died. Browning makes much of the bitter altercation between Admetos and Pheres, but, while to Euripides Pheres' thrusts only represent to his son the world's scorn of him, to Browning the scene is instrumental in the regeneration of Admetos, through holding up the mirror of sarcasm to his selfishness, as it is hardened and grown shameless in his father. So, too, Browning indicates the ennoblement of Admetos as complete before Herakles re-appears with the veiled lady, so that the demigod's temptations do not try him, but solely prove him to his wife. Browning does more for Admetos than Euripides did, more, probably, than reality would do. His idea is beautiful and modern, but it misses the unspeakable tragicalness of the original. Not satisfied even with his regenerated Admetos, Browning, at the end of his re-presentation of the Greek drama, draws a nobler husband, a happier Alkestis. But the aspiration goes to ground. We feel that it is intangible and that such a delineation would not, like that other sterner story, have outlived two thousand years. Browning diminishes what is so characteristic of the Greek drama, its arbitrariness, which probably reconciled the comparatively primitive Euripides to his mournful tragedy of marriage, in which moral feebleness murders its mate, who dies willingly, and yet in an anguish of open-eyed and despairing contempt. Euripides' Herakles is idealised by Browning. The jovial giant, glad to help an entertainer, and as glad of the wine-cup, is essentially Euripidean, and the scene of Herakles' carousal has been considered sufficient to label *Alkestis* as the satyric drama of a tetralogy. But the winning Helper of Browning is altogether a higher-hearted being, and the comparative slightness of his motive for restoring Alkestis is overpowered by the passages of admiration with which Browning irradiates the speeches and doings of the man-God. Indeed, Browning's treatment adumbrates the Christian idea rather than fuses with the Greek.

The divergences between Browning and Euripides are cumulative, for what is pure translation in the poem is literally faithful, though occasionally the translating words are just sufficiently tinged by Browning's interpretation of the characters to unite the interludes artistically with the conversations. The result of this compound of the two poets of the ancient and modern world, each so strongly idiosyncratic, is one of the most interesting and significant contrasts in literature. Each poet steals from and gives to the other, Browning catching from Euripides his pathos and simplicity, and Euripides gaining from Browning ratiocination and a profounder beauty. Browning's rendering of *Alkestis* is the greatest enrichment that ancient literature has received from modern.

Prince Hohenstiel-Schwangau, Saviour of Society, 1871 (Vol. XI.), is a casuistical study from within of Napoleon III., who was one of those moral failures which so much interested Browning's forensic mind. Browning considers him a delinquent, but one who, like Sludge and Blougram, shall not be condemned unheard. This work is Louis Napoleon's imaginary Apology for his life, and is principally interesting in evincing Browning's sympathy with every phase of thought and feeling. The monologue is a difficult one on account of its shifting standpoints. It is further complicated by sharing the speciousness of its imaginary speaker, by holding in solution Browning's real opinion on the case, and by the presence to the reader of a third figure, the historical Louis Napoleon. The narration is matched by its circumstances. Thus, the entire piece may be taken as the Emperor's soliloquy as he sits smoking in the Tuileries, through the small hours, sometime in the sixties. He has been debating whether to dispatch a courier with a letter to his 'Cousin-Duke' ('Plon-Plon,' perhaps). Meanwhile, he amuses himself by uttering, in dream shape, a defence of his life-work. This defence takes the circumstantial form of being addressed to some female haunter of

Leicester Square, as he sits with her over tea and cigars—a confused, inconsequent repetition of his earlier English exile. The fact that it is a waking dream, that 'Prince Hohenstiel-Schwangau' is really in his 'Residenz,' and only fancying himself in London, is not stated till the end. 'Prince Hohenstiel-Schwangau's' forgetfulness and mistakes in names and the mixture of circumstances are significant of the subject of the work and the manner in which that subject is treated. Browning almost, but not quite, allows us to take 'Prince Hohenstiel-Schwangau's' apology seriously, and it is a curious fact that, when the book came out, one of the first-class reviews blamed Browning for bolstering up state charlatanism. Otherwise, it scarcely need be said that Browning in no wise whitewashes the temporising, unprincipled policy of the Second Empire when he gives the special pleading by which its head may be imagined to vindicate it. The manifest sophistry and inadequacy of the plea are its strongest condemnation, and are so expressed by Browning, not explicitly, but dramatically, according to his wont. 'Prince Hohenstiel-Schwangau' unfolds the doctrine of expediency, tries to make it appear the best thing possible, and fails. For clearness, we may divide *Prince Hohenstiel-Schwangau* into two parts. Part the first (pp. 125-173) gives the grounds of the actual policy of Louis Napoleon, according to himself, *i.e.* to Browning's Louis Napoleon. 'Prince Hohenstiel-Schwangau' first defends his aim, the sustainment or 'saving' of society. He is a practical man, professing a religion which he vaunts as eminently workable. He endeavours to prove that, in his special case, the 'means' taken were left to his private inclination, provided that he attained God's 'end.' He does not pretend to be one of earth's finest minds, his 'mission' consisted in utilising his peculiar gift of making the best of what is. Great reformers are for great crises, but society's conservators or 'saviours' are invaluable in other times. 'Prince Hohenstiel-Schwangau' has balanced people's opposing tendencies for, say, twenty years, for he chiefly reverenced human life. Browning takes this opportunity of satirising the last stanzas of *Childe Harold*, and declares that the greatest nature is human nature. 'Prince Hohenstiel-Schwangau' enlarges on the advantages of imperfection, here almost identifying the defence with Browning's direct philosophy. Perhaps the adaptability of his own ideas, even in a travestied form, to Louis Napoleon's apology drew Browning to the character he is delineating. Life is too short for theories, pursues 'Prince Hohenstiel-Schwangau.' Fourierism, Comtism, Kantism need a life a century long. A tinkering policy is best suited to life's average length. There was a time—when he was 'voice and nothing more'—when he, too, breathed lofty aspirations, such as the deliverance of Italy and a democratic internal policy. He was censured for abandoning these, but it was his conviction that feeding the hungry is the essence of government that made him subordinate every thing else. Here Browning touches on Louis Napoleon's best trait, his apparently genuine care for the poor. 'Prince Hohenstiel-Schwangau' acknowledges that he only ministered to the multitudinous bodies; he let the individual souls alone, except so far as to keep the peace between them. At the conclusion of this first part of the defence, Louis Napoleon pauses, perceiving how entirely he has made his account redound to his own credit. Ostensibly to balance this, really to defend himself anew, this time obliquely, he proposes giving a fictitious autobiography, according to the Thiers-Hugo school of history. This shall represent him as embracing the fine aims and doing the grand things which he is censured for not having embraced and done. It shall also disarm the critics of his actual life by intimating the equal obloquy that would be heaped upon this imaginary 'Prince Hohenstiel-Schwangau' for being true to an impracticable ideal. 'Prince Hohenstiel-Schwangau' actually acted, on the other hand, according to 'Sagacity,' and was condemned in the spirit of his idealised self. Part the second. Louis Napoleon describes his accession as it might have been, and how, had he spared the *Coup d'Etat*, he would have been blamed for doing so. He imagines what would have been the criticism passed upon him had he established free Rome by the force, not of the sword, but of public opinion. He describes how he (in his might-have-been character) boldly forbade France ('Hohenstiel-Schwangau') its truculent joy in fighting, and kept it quiet, not by pretence of preparation for war, and so forth, but by refusing the iniquity of causeless bloodshed. In a fine passage (p. 197), Browning lauds the 'magnetic race' of France. 'Prince Hohenstiel-Schwangau' pleads his acceptance of righteous warfare, and gives a favourable sketch of his disinterestedness in the Italian undertaking. He hints that France would not have supported him without the cession of Savoy and Nice. He indulges in a final imaginative flight of patriotism in the reasons he might have alleged for refusing to have his child declared his successor. At this point, the reverie is dispersed. The 'peroration' contains what are perhaps the sincerest words yet spoken, in Louis Napoleon's expression of dissatisfaction both with his life and with its dubious justification.

Fifine at the Fair, 1872 (Vol. XI.), amid its congeries of fancies and opinions, has two prominent themes, the value of falseness or transitoriness, and the ideal meaning of marriage. These themes respectively reach the height of their expression in section cxxiv. and sections xliii., xliv. The tone of intimacy which the poem possesses makes it delightful reading to those who love Browning's mind almost more than his art. Here, and in *Red Cotton Night-Cap Country*, the poet seems to take his readers into his confidence, seems to say to them: Be my friends. As in *Prince Hohenstiel-Schwangau*, and other works, an apparently capricious and remote choice of subject brings Browning round to those truths which he loves to dwell on and to illustrate in a hundred ways. The difficulty of *Fifine at the Fair* lies in the blurring of outline between its imaginary speaker, 'Don Juan's,' words of sophistry and Browning's words of truth. Browning does not defend unlimited experiment in love, though that is the application forced by Don Juan out of the principle that souls reach truth through falsity, and the knowledge of the permanent through the fleeting. When the monologue touches on principles, we have Browning and truth, when it applies those principles to the circumstances of its supposed speaker, we have perversion. The poem is primarily dramatic, but over and above its artistically complete characterisation and story, it gives Browning's explanation—a profound and acquiescent one—of life's law of change and incompleteness. *Fifine* contains perhaps a greater wealth of variegated imagery than any other work of Browning's, while its rare and fascinating versification, its sparkling sea-side air, and its passages of impassioned imagination atone for its excessive involution.

The *Prologue*, with its brine and sunshine, is a fable of poetry as life's mimicry of immortality—

"Unable to fly, one swims!"

It also foreshows a husband and wife's separation by death, which we recognise, when we come to the

Epilogue, as binding together the three portions of the poem by their deepest idea, the lastingness of love. The extract from Molière, giving a wife's pungent suggestion to her inconstant husband of the line his defence should take, strikes the key-note of *Fifine at the Fair*, on its dramatic side. Browning's 'Don Juan' founds his plea for an extended experience with regard to women on the assumption that such experience is purely intellectual, and enhances, not deposes, the wife. He addresses his closely knit argument in defence of this position to Elvire, his wife (who is a little faded and past her prime), during an autumn evening's ramble at Pornic in Brittany. 'Don Juan' is a man of extreme æsthetic impressibility, a warm admirer of opposed types of womanhood. His intellect is as subtilising as his senses are inflammable, and he uses its refinements to try and deceive his tearful, true wife and himself as to the direction of his interest in the saucy dancer, Fifine, who has just arrived at Pornic, with a caravan, for the Fair, and whom he sees for the first time. He imagines and formulates Elvire's objections to his dangerous marital theory, and combats them. Dramatically, the monologue is Don Juan's unconscious expression of the bohemian impulse, the occasional desire for chance and change which lurks in every breast. Starting from a sympathising vindication of the gipsy vagrants' cherished lawlessness, he soon reaches the real secret of his interest in the *troupe*, the allurement of the girl in tights and spangles,

Fifine. He gives brilliant sketches of four typical women, Helen, Cleopatra, Elvire, and Fifine, basing the claim of the last on her negation of claim. That frankness, which she has, even in fraud, Don Juan later declares to be the inmost charm of the actor class to which she belongs. He pacifies Elvire by comparing her to his Rafael, Fifine to a picture-book of Doré's. He loves the peerless possession none the less that he amuses himself with the picture-book, which, at an alarm of fire, he would throw away, rushing to save his treasure. Having worked himself back into an enthusiasm for 'the wondrous wife,' he defends the philosophical truth of the assertion that beauty is in the eyes of the seer, by affirming that it is so because love is the archetypal Art, supplementing and repairing the short-comings and defects of its subject, and discerning its secret beauty. (Browning here branches into the Platonic theory of souls seeking their complementary souls.) This fructification of the lover's soul from the soul of the beloved produces a new reality for the lover, who is the sculptor, not of marble or clay, but of life. The lover gets an absolute gain, of beauty from deformity, of completeness from what was previously only suggestion. In the fact of this gain, or rather creation, Browning finds the sign-manual of immortality written on love. He looks forward to a future when the soul of the loved one shall be consciously dowered with the experience gained in the individual life of the other soul. Human beings' efforts and progress may to themselves seem self-kindled and self-centred, but are really incited by, and move towards, their lode-stars, the complementary souls. Elvire's objection that this fine talk about minds and souls covers an unconfessed interest in a certain fleshly sheath is replied to by her husband thus : 'People have to live in earthly falseness (which Fifine typifies) just as a swimmer buoys himself in water, which, were he submerged, would drown him. Truth is as vital to the soul as air to the swimmer, but just as flying is not adapted to man as he now is, so truth undiluted is impossible in the present state. The impulse to reach truth and air is necessary to life.' So far the parallel is honest, but when Don Juan proceeds to prove all experience, moral or otherwise, equally valuable to the soul's progress, he is in the sophistical region, and Browning stands aside. The sea simile concludes by making fun of the meaning and grammar of a passage in *Childe Harold*, and ridiculing Byron and his imitators for their exaltation of inanimate nature. 'Elvire may doubtless ask why women, not men, are to be her husband's educators.' Don Juan's reply, with its double pair of similitudes, contains the finest poetry in the work, notably in lxxiii., and in the comparison of women to the self-forgetting, generous dolphins in the legend of Arion. 'Elvire perhaps wonders why she, avowedly her husband's Best, cannot suffice him.' 'Because,' he ingeniously replies, 'the Fifines, like crank boats, teach 'seamanship' better than safe and steady ships.

Life is a trial of strength, whence truth is wrested by practice with the false.' Ten lines from the third of the First Book of the Odes of Horace are translated here (lxxxii.) Don Juan attributes the drift of all he has hitherto said to a dream he had in the morning, after playing Schumann, while the music itself affords him another instance of the permanence within change which is the law of art and life. He dreamed he was gazing down upon a Carnival of masks, some representing animals, some the hideousness of ignoble Age, or Youth without promise, and some, the overweening propensity which obliterates every other trait in its possessor. Then he descended among the masks to find their aggressive brutality soften down on closer inspection. He found something to sympathise with, even to admire, in those 'safeguards' of the outward men which, at a distance, had seemed repulsive. So far the 'dream' might well be Browning's own, but Don Juan adds the inevitable touch of sophistry by emphasising anew the value of every experience, inasmuch as self-knowledge is only learned through acquaintance with different beings. (Of course he is indirectly excusing his interest in Fifine.) In his dream he next saw the houses, temples, and domes dissolve, signifying to him the evanescent character of creeds, philosophies, and arts. After various transmutations, the buildings died into a great, gaunt Druid monument, such as exists at Pornic. To Browning, the monument symbolises the objective Truth and Permanence which humanity is meant to reach, through those very 'shows of sense,' which, each promising to be true and proving false, are the education which the soul—itself true and permanent—must pass through in order to arrive finally at its proper resting-place. The allusion to the *Prometheus* of Æschylus, in cxxv., whimsically compares Fifine to the Daughters of Ocean, who solaced the chained Titan. In cxxix., Don Juan overturns his sophistries by enunciating that "inconstancy means raw," that "love ends where love began," and that

> "The wanderer brings home no profit from his quest
> Beyond the sad surmise that keeping house were best
> Could life begin anew."

A less dramatic writer might have ended his work here. Not so Browning. cxxxi. prepares us for an anticlimax, which comes in the revelation of a private understanding between the husband and Fifine. There is something half pathetic in the contrast between Don Juan's last bit of philosophy and his practice. If nothing else had done so, this appropriate conclusion would prove the fallacy of his argument so far as he applied it to the justification of disloyalty. The event and its sequel are sketchily indicated in the *Epilogue*, which represents the husband deprived of the wife he was unworthy of, but rejoined to her in death by the very persistence of the love which, in life, he had exalted in word and outraged in deed.

Red Cotton Night-Cap Country, or, Turf and Towers, 1873 (Vol. XII.), is as many-sided as its maker. According as we regard it, it is a sensational novel in verse, a study of one of the anachronisms of our century's religious transition, a realistic revelation of the strange workings of certain hearts, or a delightfully roundabout book. In any case, it is a powerful, wholly unconventional instance of Browning's dramatic genius, which here invests with thought and feeling a painful story, that was tried, under the name of the Mellerio-Debacker case, in 1872, in the Court of Caen. The early part and the close of *Red Cotton Night-Cap Country* owe their chatty, familiar tone to the fact that the well-known writer, then Miss Annie Thackeray, is the story's special recipient. We learn from the poem that at 'Saint Rambert' (really Saint Aubin) on the Norman coast, where they both were in the summer of 1872, a pleasant strife arose between the poet and his friend as to whether the district was completely fitted by the appellation which Miss Thackeray playfully gave it, of 'White Cotton Night-Cap Country.' Browning characteristically insisted that some 'Red,' sin's tragic hue, lurked even in that land of drowsy-head. For some time, he plays at disappointing his listener's anticipation of any specific scarlet, thereby awakening a keener expectancy of it. When it comes, we find that the grounds for his obstinate assertion that the 'tragic bit of Red' could be extracted from the apparently humdrum somnolency of that particular corner of

France were, truly, not far to seek. In April, 1870, a curious death had occurred at Tailleville, near Saint Aubin. Monsieur Mellerio, a Parisian ex-goldsmith, son of a Southern father and French mother, had mounted to the Belvedere of his *château*, having been previously heard to say that 'angels would take him,' had plunged into the air, and, falling on the turf below, had been killed instantly. His wealth was left to the Church, with a life-interest to Madame Debacker, his seventeen-years' companion. The cousins of the deceased attempted to wrench away the property, on the plea that Mellerio was insane when he made the will, and under Madame Debacker's influence. The public disasters of 1870 postponed the lawsuit, which was only settled in July, 1872. The verdict quashed the cousins' grievance, leaving the property, as willed, to the Church, and to the lady, sometime adventuress, who had so long lived with the late Mellerio, and whose absolute fidelity had only been equalled by his to her. Many facts of Mellerio's life came out in the trial, some ugly, and one horrible yet almost grand. This was the incident of his burning off his hands to the wrists to 'purify his past,' and to express his remorse for his mother's death, which he had been made to believe his profligacy and extravagance had induced. These facts (which most writers would have considered too strange for fiction) Browning pondered, till he was able to spell out an answer to the enigma, and to realise, and pronounce sane, a man who could live in avowed sin with a woman not his wife, and yet entertain the childish ignorance of imagining that the Virgin would suspend gravitation for his special assurance of her omnipotence and grace. It should be mentioned that Mellerio, on the day of his death, had evidently expected that a miracle would be worked in his favour by one of the three wonder-working images of France, *La Délivrande*, whose church and establishment were two miles from Tailleville. The only difference between the statements of the poem and what appeared in the actual evidence consists in an unimportant diversity of dates, and an entire change of the names, both of persons and places, *Paris* and *the coast of Normandy* alone remaining intact.

Red Cotton Night-Cap Country is so much the most quickly read of Browning's longer works, and is so rapidly comprehensible that it is needless to retrace its successive stages here. In it, Browning shows himself for the first time mindful of the novelist's art of stimulating curiosity to the end. The two images of the title round off and illustrate every incident and reflection. Almost as frequent are the references to gems, lapidaries' similes which befit the ex-jeweller's story. The idea of 'turf and towers,' besides its manifest suitability to the catastrophe between the garden and the Belvedere, continuously points a moral. As the poem proceeds, the metaphor grows into an elaborate allegory, side by side with the story. 'Turf' symbolises self-indulgence and wrong-doing, while by 'towers' is signified the life of duty. The towers, 'outline sad, severe,' look forbidding enough in youth, when the necessity for soldier-like manning of their ramparts seems (as low-minded religious teachers would leave men to infer) fifty years distant. For the present, at all events, it is pleasanter to erect a tent or pavilion on the tempting turf, for, doubtless, the towers can be mounted later. The 'tent' represents the fatal course of compromise, or 'general utility,' which that devil-saint, Sganarelle,[1] is always ready to recommend to any one who will listen. 'Léonce Miranda' (Mellerio) began life by trying to shrewdly balance God and sin. It is needless to say that he failed in the endeavour. The second half of his life was spent in attempting to unite God and sin, and to compound for guilt by penances. Because 'Clara Muhlhausen' (Madame Debacker) was a divorced wife, 'Miranda' was too devout a son of the Church to marry her, though he transgressed a plainer law than the Church's by living with her without marriage. His religion was a superstition, as his Divinity was a 'Queen of Angels' in lace and crown. Still, it personified conscience to him, and it was not his credulity, but his half-hearted action, that wrecked him morally. The sublime bit of his life was when he threw himself, his struggling and unsatisfied conscience, his doubt, and the doubt of the world upon the supernatural being whom he had never succeeded in realising sufficiently, and,

---

[1] See Molière's *Don Juan*, and other plays.

with a passionate appeal for acceptance, put his trust and the power of 'The *Ravissante*' (*La Délivrande*) to the test. In Browning's eyes, the deed was not religious mania, but perfectly reasonable. Given the belief, or half-belief, which was all that Miranda's foolish head could hold, and there was something heroic in risking his life on the promise of its efficacy. Just because such a distracted deed, such a folly, was possible, Browning pronounces the religion which incited it, though 'decomposing,' dangerous still, not, as some say, an extinct bugbear. This is the explanation of the allegory of 'the partial-ruin,' which Browning uses early in the poem. He counsels the timely demolition of whatever threatens to fall on any living head, letting the picturesqueness of the 'ruins' be a secondary consideration. The reactionary wave of Catholicism, so perceptible in France in the early seventies, doubtless accentuated Browning's animadversion. At the same time, it would be grotesquely untrue to regard *Red Cotton Night-Cap Country* as principally a protest against Romanism. To Browning, the worst evil doers of the story are not the foolish thinkers, but those, the 'Parish-priest' and the 'Mother of the Convent' of 'The *Ravissante*' who condoned 'Miranda's' sin for the sake of his offerings. The mother of Léonce, 'Madame Miranda,' is likewise condemned for countenancing that most pernicious rule of life, 'general utility.' Browning only judges 'Miranda' and his poor, broken life from 'Miranda's' own standpoint. It is not because he mistook 'The *Ravissante*' for God, and 'Clara' (Madame Debacker) for love's representative, but because he tried to compromise between, and, that failing, to unite immorality and religion that he is found wanting. 'Clara' is a less vivid shape to Browning's readers than the feminine 'Miranda,' though Browning himself regards her parasitic character as the more readily definable. She is a third-rate figure of steel coated with wax. 'Miranda' was constant to his love, generous, and, at least, distinguished from his mediocre mental equals by carrying out his fatuous logic to the point of burning off his hands in expiation, of leaping from a tower to testify and assure his faith.

The characters of the story, which at first sight may seem tawdry, and certainly do not rise to heroic simplicity, aptly represent something of the complicated and dim uneasiness prevalent in the age to which they belong. Still, there lingers the impression of a kind of sophism about the work, a making of the artistic worse appear the better, a wilful choice of inferiorities, much as though the glorious creativeness of *Caponsacchi* and *Pompilia* were deliberately wasted on the composition of a *Ring and the Book* in which Pietro and Violante Comparini should figure as protagonists.

Aristophanes' Apology; including a Transcript from Euripides; being the Last Adventure of Balaustion, 1875 (Vol. XIII.), is, like the poem to which it is in part a sequel, largely in honour of the third great Attic tragedian. Nine years have passed since Balaustion saved her life and gained her husband by reciting *Alkestis* from the steps of the Heraklæum at Syracuse. The Peloponnesian War is over, and Athens' Long Walls have been razed, to the sound of joyful music. Balaustion and her husband, Euthukles, are sorrowfully quitting the 'dead' city of their adoption, the city of the poet who links them to the divine. At every sunset-close, as the galley bears them to Rhodes, Euthukles writes from Balaustion's dictation her memorial of Athens, and of its best friend, Euripides. Balaustion cannot awake her memories without associating them with a discourse, cognate to their subject, that took place a year earlier between herself and Aristophanes. That discourse she · will revive, for it is significant now that it can be interpreted by the light of subsequent events.

Another story from Plutarch is embedded in this second record of Balaustion. The Phokian, mentioned in the Life of Lysander as having averted the demolition of Athens by recalling to the Spartans a Chorus from Euripides' *Elektra*, is assumed to be Balaustion's husband. Indeed, this sequel to *Balaustion's Adventure* is so adroitly founded on historical facts, that its art seems nature, and the result an inevitable coincidence of the story of declining Athens with Balaustion, and of both with Euripides. All things that make for verisimilitude seem to have worked together for Browning in this setting of his translation of *Herakles Mainomenos*. 'Setting,' however, is too subordinate a term to describe Browning's surrounding of Euripides' tragedy, so strenuous and organic is 'Aristophanes' Apology' and the later experience of Balaustion, the one as virile and intellectual as the other is lyric and womanly.

The 'Last Adventure of Balaustion' was her hearing of 'Aristophanes' Apology,' and occurred on this wise. One night, a year before Aigispotamoi (I follow Browning's spelling in order to act as a finger-post to the poem), Aristophanes and his rabble rout had burst into Balaustion's quiet home. It had been the day of the representation of Aristophanes' *Thesmophoriazusæ*, parodying and ridiculing Euripides, and also the day when the news reached Athens of Euripides' death in Macedonia. Balaustion was known to be the tragedian's most prominent admirer in Athens, and Aristophanes, flown with wine, had been struck, after his triumph-night feast at the State's expense, with the idea of half insolently, half sympathetically, calling upon Euripides' spiritual executrix, the cloud left rosy with the departed sunset of the poet. Intrusions upon household privacy were frequent in Athens, and we need only turn to the interruption and conclusion of Plato's 'Banquet' to find what perhaps supplied the hint for the *mise en scène* and theme of *Aristophanes' Apology*. Abashed by the purity and severity of the Rhodian wife, chorus, choragus, flute-boys, and dancing-girls slink away, leaving the Wine-lees-poet alone with his hosts. There ensues a long conversation, which is for many pages Aristophanes' defence of his comedies, and afterwards Balaustion's refutation of each of his arguments. Challenged to defend her poet, Balaustion knows no better way than, following an example set by Sophokles, to read aloud the autograph work Euripides gave her, which she and Euthukles were about to have read in commemoration, not vindication, had not Aristophanes broken in upon the rite. Aristophanes' better nature is for the second time evoked, and he comments, after the reading, on the difference between himself and Euripides, in a graver mood than he has hitherto assumed. The ground of his defence broadens and, for that very reason, becomes even more sophistical. He tries to quiet the still, small voice by asserting that artistic perfection surpasses elevation of character, and that he did well to perfect his own bent—as if he had not cultivated a bent towards muck and mire and towards 'taking stand on lower ground than truth'! His moral baseness, not the limitation of his genius, is the cause of Balaustion's quarrel against him. The burlesque vein presently reasserts itself, though not before he has improvised a rhapsodical chant, almost the one touch in Browning's Aristophanes of that Shelley-like sensibility to beauty which is as marked a characteristic of the teacher of the *Clouds* as his ribaldry and scurrility. Through the lyric words breaks, with a strong rebound, Aristophanes' intense sense of the ludicrous, that essentially Aristophanic quality which Browning almost sinks in the earlier part of the Apology, when Aristophanes is pressing upon hostile auditors his demand to be taken seriously.

The triumph of the poem is its imaginative creation of the man, Aristophanes. Browning is as true to the extant comedies and the references of contemporaries as to his own conception and his prejudice against the lampooner of Euripides. Every page of the *Apology* is saturated with references to the plots, characters, and mud-pellets of Aristophanes' works.[1] That laughing-stock, Euripides according to the comedies, with the caricatured lines

> My tongue hath sworn—my mind remains unsworn [2]

and

> Who knows if Life is Death . . .
> And Death is Life ? [3]

appears throughout the *Apology* side by side with the true shape of the retired, ascetic poet, who so much exasperated his reviler by not noticing his abuse. The poem is full of contrasts,—between the baldhead bard and austere Balaustion, between the heroic simplicity of *Herakles* and the sophistical complexities of the 'Apology,' between the two methods, comic and tragic—opposed systems of working for the social benefit by depicting the lofty or making game of the vile, between Aristophanes' attacks on Euripides as

[1] The volume on Aristophanes in *Ancient Classics for English Readers* is helpful towards understanding many of the allusions.

[2] Cp. Eur. *Hippolytus*, 608-612 with Aris. *Thesmophoriazusæ*, 275 and *Frogs*, 101, 102, and 1471.

[3] Cp. Eur. *Polyidus*, fr. 639, and *Phrixus*, fr. 830 with Aris. *Frogs*, 1082 and 1477.

Athens' enemy and the comment thereupon afforded by the fact that a line from Euripides saved the Akropolis, while to the music of Aristophanes' chorus the Piræan bulwarks were demolished. A deeper contrast lies in the universal meaning of the poem behind its elaborate delineation of Athenian life. It is focused in that brilliant illustration from the game of kottabos (pp. 232, 233) which represents the conflict between idealism and naturalism, between moral selection and all-inclusive experience. The vitality of the poem is not to be found in its welding of scholarship with imagination, nor even in its creation of Balaustion, Pompilia's kinswoman and the most cultivated heroine in literature, but in Browning's contribution through it to the eternal debate: Shall flesh rule me? or spirit and flesh alternately? or together? or shall spirit rule flesh? On the artistic side, Browning sympathises with Aristophanes' defence; on the moral side, he vividly realises his position; and he yearns, like his own Euripides, towards the degraded Titan with his inextinguishable genius. Yet what the argument, nothing if not ethical, actually resolves itself into is, on Aristophanes' side, pleas, which he feels to be dubious, for his lies, bestialities, and determination to raise a laugh at no matter whom nor at what expense, and, on Balaustion's, a confutation of Aristophanes by comparing him with Euripides, and a confutation of his pleas, which is focused in the lines—

"know,—worst sophistry
Is when man's own soul plays its own self false."

In *Aristophanes' Apology*, as elsewhere, we find how simple is the substructure of Browning's most labyrinthine edifices. His art is so much more complicated than his philosophy.

Herakles is as much a sequel to *Alkestis* as is Balaustion's later adventure to her earlier one. The sequence of Euripidean victories is perfect in every detail, down to its being the self-same Kaunian ship and captain that now convey Balaustion to Rhodes.

Herakles, the jubilant champion and labourer for men, cannot live without defeat. Life claims her due, and the heavy payment comes about thus. While Herakles performs his last labour, plucking Kerberos from Haides, his wife, sons, and earthly father are turned out of their palace by the usurper, Lukos, and now await death at his hands. Herakles reappears and slays Lukos, but Heré's vengeance is not fully wreaked. She sends madness to Herakles, and, in his frenzied state, he kills his boys, taking them for his task-master's children. His wife, too, he slays. When madness departs, despair and shame take possession of Herakles. The kingly, grateful Theseus befriends him in this desolation, and, at Theseus' bidding, Herakles, his faith in God outliving his rejection of Olympian legends, accepts the sorrowfulness of his life, with greater bravery than his most daring labours evoked. His discipline and patience are the sublimest picture in Euripides.

The Inn Album, 1875 (Vol. XII.), though in narrative form, is properly an undeveloped drama, and, save in the scene between Ottima and Sebald in *Pippa Passes*, its dramatic intensity is unequalled. Browning takes for subject, not 'the healthy natures of a grand epoch,'[1] but a story from modern life, of crime and moral distortion, suggesting melodrama, but raised by his treatment to tragedy. So far the poem resembles *Red Cotton Night-Cap Country*, but the speculative background, the meditative atmosphere of the earlier work are absent from this one. Instead of feeling the presence of the author, praising, blaming, sympathising, sometimes momentarily identifying himself with one or other of his characters, we find an absolutely concentrated treatment, which leaves no space for discursiveness. Browning's own vision of life is curtained for the nonce, and the dramatic half of his mind dominates, obliterating the philosophical half, so far as we may call that obliteration which is really metamorphism. No embryonic motives, no instincts still waiting in the cavity of consciousness to be born and named, but human nature, fully grown, manifesting itself in action, and begetting its fate, is the subject of *The Inn Album*. Throughout, there is not a line of soliloquy. Browning forbids himself any self-revealment of his characters which is not modified by the presence of a hearer or hearers. The drama is an internal and external tragedy, and the outcome and conclusion of a former one. The actors, intensely distinct and clear-cut, but all nameless, are four—an oldish man, a woman, a

[1] Preface to *Strafford*, 1837.

young man, and a girl. Though the girl is instrumental to the plot, psychologically, emotionally, the play lies between the other three.

This tragedy of the passions is in eight scenes, or half-acts, most of which take place (a contrast grotesquely humorous) in the stuffy parlour of an inn. The progress of the piece may be summarised thus . . . I. (Lord ——, a too accomplished card-player, and a libertine 'of much newspaper-paragraph,' has for a year past attached himself to a young fellow, the son of a self-made millionaire. The older man, whose life has been a failure, notwithstanding his large measure of ability and what must be called personal magnetism, crossed the young one's path when the latter was suffering from a disappointment in love for which he purposed abandoning the world to misanthropise in a distant solitude. Induced by his new friend to give up this idea, he became superficially initiated by him in worldliness, and is now about to marry a rich cousin.) The poem opens in the village inn, where the youth has been spending the eve of his visit to the country mansion of his betrothed in playing cards with his evil genius, who had hoped to indemnify himself by one night's success for his approaching loss in the marriage of his 'pupil.' The first speaker is the older man. He asks for the inn album, wherein to reckon the result of the night's play. The reckoning proves him to be the loser, to the extent of ten thousand pounds. The youth offers to cancel the debt, which he knows would prove an almost impossible one to the needy man. Lord —— affects to scout the idea, replying to the well-meaning tactlessness of his half-unwilling admirer in words partly sardonic, partly conciliatory. II. The youth, still troubled at the thought of taking the impoverished lord's money, sets to wondering why it is that one so much older, so infinitely abler, should be without any of those substantial goods which he himself possesses in superabundance. His companion acknowledges his failure to be due to a fatal woman. Then he tells, in an impenitent, ignorant way ('ignorant' in the sense applied to it on pp. 276, 278 of *case-hardened* or *narrow-hearted*) the story of how, four years ago, he won—and betrayed—a young girl's love. His victim only leapt out of her fascination, her captivity, when he disclosed that he had not intended marriage. Her wrath surprised him into offering it, whereupon she further astonished him by refusing. He had destroyed the love he had created. The enormity of his offence seems, even to himself, to demand some attempt at palliation, so he lamely professes that he originally intended to act honourably, had not circumstances hurried him wrong. He dimly blames his victim's very perfection of surface for hiding the soul which so removed her from the women of his experience. Since her disdainful rejection of his offer of marriage, her life has passed from his ken. One fact only is known to him—that in a month she had married a country clergyman. Now comes one of the piercing flashes of insight into this tragedy of souls. The speaker acknowledges that, since the affair he has been describing, his life has withered, and every thing has gone wrong; yet he ignores the significance of the nemesis that has pursued him. The man's grand opportunity (and we know how great is Browning's sense of the value of life's crises as chances for character) was the revelation of a lofty and, till then, pure woman. She loved him, and might have been his saviour. Instead, he blasphemed his opportunity, defiling what he should have worshipped and cherished.

> "I hate who *would not understand*,
> Let me *repair things*."

The blind heart that utters that is as much fool as knave, as we shall presently see more completely. Meanwhile his listener, true to youthfulness, does not feel the tragedy much, till, as it soon will, it crosses his own life. Encouraged, however, by his companion's confidence, he tells how he too met his 'wonder of a woman.' By this phrase, both instinctively describe her, who, unknown to them, is one and the same. She had met the young Oxonian during the time of her captivation by the older man, and had refused his honest devotion—"she was another's." When, later, the youth heard that his ideal had married, he thought it was to the man she loved. Still, she stands to him for all love, all loveliness, his affianced cousin being merely his cousin. III. The men vacate the stage for awhile,

and the woman and the girl enter. The latter has
lately been disturbed by a vague fear that she and
her betrothed have mistaken 'easy ignorance' of each
other for knowledge. She has sent for the married
woman to decide the case, and, after seeing him,
pronounce judgment on the lover. For four years
the girl has seen nothing of her old friend, whom
conjugal happiness has, she fancies, engrossed. Who
then so able to decide on a question regarding
marriage? The girl, like her cousin, possesses a large
share of insensibility, or she would discern the woman's
terrible world-weariness. In easy assumption of the
life of bliss led by the parson's wife, she rattles on,
till even her stupidity is shivered by her interlocutor.
Before more can be inquired, the older woman has
despatched her to fetch the lover. IV. The sorrowful lady is alone, when, all unwittingly, he, the fifty-
years-old libertine, enters, who was the cause of her
shame. There they stand, hate fronting hate in
words of ice and fire. The man, detesting the incarnation of that image which has seemed to dog
each subsequent false step of his life, taunts her with
her marriage, for which he guessed a base, shallow-
hearted motive. Her reply contains another of
Browning's flashes of insight into human nature.
When, four years ago, she started back in horror
from the miscreant's commonplace proposal of making
her 'amends by marriage,' eclipsed self-respect re-
dawned in her consciousness of her own capacity for
contempt. Browning regards that capacity for great

scorn as the sure pledge of a future, redeemable and infinite. She who could feel so was not utterly lost nor degraded. This being so, she could live on, choosing a life penitential in the extreme. She married a purblind, drudging parish-priest, old and poor, yet desiring a woman's help in doling out his sterile ministrations in a sterile parish. Among brutalised people, she has endured an existence of drear apathy. No 'human lucid laugh' has penetrated it, and to-day's hearing of one had almost forbidden her return to bondage, till her betrayer's reappearance checked such impulse. For reply, the man tells her she never loved him if she loathes him now. She controverts this, in words that, over its grave, recall the dead enthusiasm. Then the man's cynicism half breaks up. Throwing himself before her, he cries to her to redeem his life by uniting hers with it to the end. He strives to excuse his doubt of love, he assails her soul with subtle temptation, finest flattery, himself for the moment seeming to struggle with his own evil. The passage is tragical in the contrast between what is genuine in the man's appeal and the woman's hurling back of all of it. She only hears in it a bidding to break faith with the husband whom she has rightly kept uninformed of her story of woe. She is deriding the man, changing his revived ardour into malignancy, when the youth enters. V. The young man and she recognise each other. To his whirl of consciousness, her presence together with the older man's attitude look like plotted villainy.

His rash invective she silences by explaining the situation sufficiently to solemnly warn him against the 'friend' who has ruined her life and would ruin his. (And now the older man, with the luck against him, and egged on by the woman's scorn and disbelief, and the young man, his now undeceived dupe's threats, prepares to play a last card. He conceives the double purpose of ridding himself of his money debt and revenging his rebuff from the woman, by writing in the Album what he calls the price of his keeping silence on the past to her husband. This he sends her into the adjoining room to read. The price of his silence is that she shall accept a frankly dishonouring offer if such be made her by the younger man.) VI. Alone with the youth, the 'Adversary' traduces the woman, predicting, in proof of her infamy, that she will accept the proposal which he recommends the young man to make her. The fee for the lesson in womankind that he represents himself as giving, if found correct, may fairly be, he urges, the remission of the ten thousand pounds. VII. The evil one retires to await success, and the lady re-enters. (While in the other room, she has taken a poison always kept by her against some such need.) She comprehends what has passed during her absence, and, in words that have death's calmness upon them, disperses the calumnies of her foe. The young man's reply to her, unknowing though he yet is of the threat in the Album, is a generous, selfless offer to her of his life's service. This is one of the grandest dramatic passages in Browning's works. In its few minutes, the youth turns man, all his callowness done away with. Every rag of a boy's conventionality is scattered to the winds in the equal delicacy and directness of the speech. He has offered her his hand for ever. She takes it, knowing, as he does not, what 'for ever' means. When the enemy returns, even he is taken aback at the apparent success of his scheme. He little imagines the pact come to by natures so unlike his. With loathsome compliment, he congratulates the couple, but is interrupted by the dying woman, who reads to her champion the writing in the Album. For fitting comment, the younger man springs at the villain, and strangles him. VIII. The woman dies, but not till she has falteringly written what will vindicate her deliverer's conduct. There is silence in the room. Outside, a laughing voice is heard. It is that of the girl, to whom dreadful news has to be broken by the grave survivor, saved as he is from doing her the supreme indignity of marriage without love.

Pacchiarotto and how he worked in Distemper: with other Poems, 1876 (Vol. XIV.), is Browning's first work in the serio-grotesque key which, on and off, distinguishes his penultimate period. The poet's personal robustness runs riot in the present volume. Four of the poems, *At the " Mermaid," House, Shop,* and the *Epilogue* repudiate poetic self-delineation, yet in these very pieces Browning is self-delineative as to his poetic methods and principles. Such a paradox comes naturally from the apostle of paradoxes.

Prologue (*A Wall* in the *Selections, Second Series*, 1880) is a little reverie, induced by watching the pulsation and flutter of wall foliage. That common sight, which mysteriously stimulates most imaginations, is full of supersensual suggestiveness to Browning.

Of Pacchiarotto, and how he worked in Distemper is a true story, frolicsomely told, of the Sienese painter of the early sixteenth century whose personality it is hard to disentangle from that of his contemporary fellow-townsman, Pacchia. The poem, with its sportive rhymes, is a merry quirk, abounding in the liberty of power. Browning has frequently insisted that a man's wisdom is no more than he needs to shape his own course aright, and he enjoys this opportunity of showing how ill advised meddling and dreams of social perfectibility brought to grotesque grief a reformer who would have done better to stick to his paint-pot. A similar idea was gravely expressed in *The Boy and the Angel*. The reformed reformer, the Abbot, and the corpse urge no selfish letting-be, but a strenuous doing of one's individual best towards earth's amelioration, chastened by a full acceptance of the unconquerable unevenness of what Browning[1] calls this 'Rehearsal,' life. Browning tacks on to *Pacchiarotto* proper a roistering mockery of his reviewers, 'in the drabs, blues, and yellows.'

[1] Cp. Epictetus, *Encheiridion*, XVII.

The next to naming of a special critic, and the character of his threatened punishment remind us that Browning has been recently saturating himself in Aristophanes.

At the "Mermaid" disclaims the idea of directly personal utterance having any place in a dramatic poet's works, and disavows a poetic leadership founded on any pandering to the taste of the public for personal disclosures. Browning puts on Shakspere's mantle to cover the haughtiness of a declaration of independence all his own. 'Last king' is, of course, Byron, whom Browning so constantly belabours. The expression "threw Venus" refers to the best throw, called 'Venus' (thrice six), in dice.

House, like *At the "Mermaid,"* disallows any spirit in poetic utterance but the dramatic one. The quotation is from Wordsworth's sonnet on the Sonnet. Neither by mind nor art was Browning fitted to form a triad with the sonnet masters, Shakspere and Wordsworth.

Shop condemns those who write solely for profit—of money or fame. Its striking and noble protest equally applies to all men with muck-rakes, who can look no way but downwards.

Pisgah - Sights. I. suggests the insight into the meaning of life, and the acquiescence in its apparent evils, which a dying man may have. II. resembles *An Epistle of Karshish* in representing the paralysis of action, and untimely spiritual precocity, that a man would have did his 'Pisgah-Sight' come while he was still toiling through earth's wilderness.

Fears and Scruples is a parable of theistic faith on trial. Its personifications give it an affecting inwardness.

Natural Magic consists of two stanzas which transpose, as is the case with allegories, the natural order of thought. No lover needs an interpretation of love's 'natural magic.'

Magical Nature tells of the soul's beauty that age cannot wither. Note the lovely versification of these companion poems, especially the smooth opulence of the line—

'Jewel at no mercy of a moment in your prime.'

Bifurcation is one of Browning's most remarkable short poems. Simple enough in expression, it is as mysterious as a transcript from life should be. It is, like *Fears and Scruples*, a riddle, only in this case the answer is withheld. Browning seems to condemn the woman for following a counsel of prudence instead of the ardour of the heart, and the condemnation would be characteristic, but perhaps he both forbears to judge, and would have us forbear.

Numpholeptos, in natural proximity to *Bifurcation*, is high-fantastical in its scenic circumstance. Essentially, it describes a man 'seized by a nymph' who sets him tasks. He journeys forth on his quests, to return inevitably stained with travelling. The immaculate She will not forgive these stains. Idle, useless, and ignorant of life, she expects the impossible, weighing her worshipper by the unreal standard of her own cloistered virtue. (Happily, the unsympathising and ungenerous being, 'hearted' in the white centre of the prism, is *not* a superior young woman, but only a 'nymph'!)

Appearances, a dramatic miniature, tells how life is made 'poor' or 'rich,' not by externals, patent to all, but by the hidden history of the heart.

St. Martin's Summer is instinct with a delicious shiver of only half-metaphorical ghostliness. The speaker deprecates the idea of formally entering upon a new love. He has, and perhaps the lady he addresses has too, buried loves whose ghosts are unlaid. Friendliness, better than love, suits such autumnal creatures as he and she. Yet he is congratulating himself on virtually eluding the ghosts, when suddenly they assert their reality, mocking and pulverising the present.

Hervé Riel, the grand ballad every one knows, seems to belong to the same inspiration as *Good News from Ghent*. Neither of Browning's most popular poems has an English theme. *Hervé Riel* was originally published in the *Cornhill Magazine*, March, 1871, that Browning might contribute the sum (£100) given for it to the fund for sending food to Paris after the siege.

A Forgiveness is the strongest poem in the *Pacchiarotto* volume. It is one of the four or five 'sample' pieces that Browning said he "should not object to be judged by." The narrative is given by a powerful and implacable Spaniard, in seeming confession to a monk, once the man who wronged him. It is no common story of a wife's dishonour and a husband's revenge, for the husband scorned to award 'hate's punishment' to her who had evoked only 'contempt's.' He let her act a part, not live, beside him, for three long years. Then she told him that jealousy of his absorption in state affairs, not passion for the wretched moth, her lover, had been her motive. She loved, still loves, her husband. This avowal raises her out of his contempt—into his hate. He offers her a poisoned dagger. She uses it on herself, assured that in revenge, hate is quenched, that, dead, she will be loved 'as erst.' It now only remains to annihilate the monk. Short as the poem is, its characterisation is absolutely complete. Nothing could more effectively express the stoic Spaniard, his code and ideal, than the measured punctiliousness, the gradation from contempt to hatred, the self-command, the unhasting, unresting vindictiveness, and the exquisite torture devised for his enemy.

Cenciaja tracks the reference (in Shelley's *Cenci*, V., 4) that weighed with Clement VIII. to seal Beatrice Cenci's doom. It is a story of the corrupt Church of the year 1600, avenged, as Browning puts it, in 1870. The poem evidences Browning's scrupulous love of winding up every loose end of a story, reminding us of that more famous record of the miscarriages, and final vindication, of justice, as given in the last section of *The Ring and the Book*.

Filippo Baldinucci on the Privilege of Burial is a grimly comic narration of what befel Jews in Florence. Up to stanza xxxvi., the story is fact, as related by Filippo Baldinucci (n. 1624—ob. 1696) in his voluminous *History of Design*. Baldinucci's vulgar imbecility is racily rendered, and in telling contrast with the patient dignity of the Jews.

Epilogue contains more of such sturdy, vigorous sentiments as appeared in *At the "Mermaid."* Browning now addresses the public rather than the critics. His turning of the tables on those who swear by the classics they do not read is caustic raillery. Stanza xiv. is a piece of suggestive criticism. Again Browning refuses to make his 'house' his 'shop,' again he gibes at Byron, again he tells us, what we know so well, that he himself brews 'stiff drink' and his 'vineyard' is

'Man's thoughts and loves and hates.'

The Agamemnon of Æschylus, 1877 (Vol. XIII.), is Browning's third transcript from the Greek. Every one remembers the outline of what forms the main subject of this Drama, the story of Agamemnon's death—how he returned from Ilion to Argos in company with Cassandra, and how Clytemnestra, his wife, killed them both. The *Agamemnon* contains, in common with all Greek plays, but here in surpassing measure, so almost infinite a number of meanings, so inexhaustible a store of ageless life, that one only wishes Browning had illuminated this first, this form-creating Drama, as he did the *Alkestis*, with such another wise and brilliant commentary. Then we might have had the hymns concerning Iphigenia and Helen as detached from the platitudes of the chorus, and from the speeches of Cassandra, agonising under Apollo's spell, and of Clytemnestra, after the deed, 'magnificent in sin,' like Ottima and Lady Macbeth, though greater and worse than either. Then, too, Browning could have impressed upon his readers how shallow is the conventional misnomer of fatalism for Æschylus' supreme sense of retribution, of Erinnyes. Æschylus is mankind's majestic prophet of the certainty of punishment for crime, and of the far-reaching consequences of action, and he is at his most prophetic in the *Agamemnon*. Itself the story of the consequences of a precedent event (the staining of the house of Tantalus by the horrible meal of Atreus), it is only the commencement of another continuous action, the first play of the *Orestea*. Its truth to nature combining with an artistically rounded, unmistakable presentment of retributive justice makes the *Orestea* a mine of teaching. Æschylus is no less certain than an old Jewish lawgiver that the sins of the fathers must be expiated by the children unto the third and fourth generation. At the same time, he shows enough immediate cause of these visitations to satisfy the demand for justice to individuals and for human volition as well as divine vengeance and its impelling force. Agamemnon dies, not merely because the unsated demon sits on his roof demanding fulfilment of Thyestes' curse, but because he sacrificed his daughter to his self-will and ambition. These are the inner, ethical causes, but on the surface appear what to the unthinking are causes enough for Agamemnon's murder, in Clytemnestra's jealousy of Cassandra, her desertion of Agamemnon for Ægisthus, and their joint scheme to destroy him. Neither does Æschylus omit the favourite Greek moral, the injury wrought on character by too great prosperity. The Greeks preferred a mixture of failure with prosperity, instead of universal success, and Æschylus gives effect to this feeling in the case of the King of men by his 'treading,' though reluctantly, 'the purple to his death.'[1]

Both the excellences and defects of Browning's translation are only appreciable by scholars, and, on account of its daring, enthusiastic truthfulness line by line to the text, by them alone can the greatness of Browning's toil and its result be valued. The mode, or, at all events, the effect, of the rendering of *Agamemnon*, differs from that of *Alkestis* and *Herakles*. Its key is in the preface, where Browning lays down as his axiom of translation literalness, supporting it by many a good reason. But when he speaks of translating 'the very turn of each

[1] *Pauline*,' i. 26—an interesting reference when we compare the dates of *Pauline* and this Transcript.

phrase,' we cannot help thinking of what is the result of turning foreign idioms into literal English. This is too much what he has tried to do with Æschylus. He goes to the roots of both languages in order to match the Greek word, with the result that he not infrequently translates according to the word, not according to the sense. He seems to ignore how much the meaning of words depends on the associations that perhaps the English word has quite lost and is therefore, at the present time, no real equivalent. The determination to achieve etymological exactitude has here and there made fidelity to the spirit of the original o'er-leap itself. The letter killeth in

"things there be, *one barks*,"
When no man harks" (p. 289),

and

"I was rightly of this slaughter *stitch-man*" (p. 352).

Then again, Browning acts well in preserving the ruggedness of Æschylus, but ill when he overlays it with words and phrases which from their oddity give an added harshness. Inversions peculiar to Browning prevent the translation from being what a translation should be, as far as possible a transparent medium. If we compare the openings of the first two speeches with a literal but unliterary 'crib,' such as Bohn's, we find how Browning has added difficulty to that which had too much. He would seem to have been committed to this occasionally artificial fidelity before he translated the tragedy, otherwise it is hard to imagine how his dramatic imagination, which stood him in such stead when he was realising to himself Alkestis and Herakles, should have permitted the flat rendering of certain lines of Clytemnestra's and of the last words of the tragic Cassandra. Doubtless, a less intimate tie connects Browning's sympathy with Æschylus than with Euripides. It seems ungracious to disparage aught in a version wherein genius, scholarship, and the most special qualifications in Browning's enormous resources of word and rhymes have done their all but triumphant. One rather turns to those innumerable instances where the native beauty of the poem is accentuated by Browning. Tact in words is a translator's genius, and, with certain egregious exceptions, Browning's rendering abounds in it. The approximations to the Greek measures both in the dramatic and choric passages are very successful. Certain lines, especially from the lyrics, must hereafter for ever cancel all other translations whatsoever. For examples, take a line from Clytemnestra's imagination-picture of the victorious Greeks

'In the spear-captured Troic habitations'

and this of Helen in Troy—a history in a brace of lines—

"There she stands silent! meets no honour—no
Shame—sweetest still of things gone long ago"

and the accuracy, infinitely superior to 'elegances' of translation, of

"Ah, Linos, say—ah, Linos, song of wail!
But may the good prevail!"

La Saisiaz : The Two Poets of Croisic, 1878 (Vol. XIV.), are the poems, dissociated enough in mood and theme, which form Browning's next volume.

La Saisiaz is prefaced by three verses (reprinted as *Pisgah-Sights*, III. in *Selections, Second Series*) which, coming as they are imagined to do, from a just disembodied soul, sound the key-note of the entire work—faith in a better life after death. The earth-bound man utters darkling faith, but the freed spirit, joyful assurance. The relation between this prelude and *La Saisiaz* is very beautiful.

'La Saisiaz' is the name of a villa among the mountains of Savoy, where the sad incident occurred which suggested the poem. A valued friend, who was staying with the poet and his sister, died there suddenly on September 14th, 1877. Without warning, death's chill and blank effaced the gaiety of the holiday, the apparent security of the life, the sympathy of the companionship. The mystery of death, never so earnestly interrogated as after a shock of suddenness like this, turned the poet's reflections from his loss to the problem whether the great change means extinction. The subject of immortality had, a few days previously, been discussed between the friends, and Browning, climbing where they were to have ascended together, speaks out his train of thought, as though to the 'Dear and True' who is no longer beside him. Browning's

structure of belief entirely rests on two postulates,
the existence of the soul and the existence of God.
He attempts to prove neither, because *to him* they are
self-evident. This point of individual testimony is
dwelt upon. Browning takes self (as in *Rabbi Ben
Ezra*) as the centre of its universe and the judge of
all phenomena, and self-development as self's tendency
and eventual aim. To grant these two personalities,
the subjective and the objective, or soul and God, is
an enormous assumption, though Browning never
questions either. This is not because he shrinks from
probing for truth, but because he was born a poet,
and therefore a mystic. Accordingly, he affirms that,
to the extent of his only two assumptions, he *knows*[1]
that "which passeth knowledge." All doctrine in-
ferential therefrom is matter for 'surmise,' and that
is the peculiar province of Browning's searching
intellect. The basis of his belief in immortality is
that life is only explicable as probation. It is the
inexplicableness, rather than the injustice, of life for
which he needs the hope of a different hereafter.
Yet, looking at life, he decides that, were its conditions final, evil outweighs good. The positivist's
social immortality is inconsistent with the personal
soul's conception of the personal God. Successively,
Browning tries life, as he knows it, with every key
but that of probation and immortality, and finds that

---

[1] Cp. Abt Vogler's—

"The others may reason and welcome ; 'tis we musicians" (poets)
"*know.*"

not one of them opens the door. Afterwards, he shifts his ground, and approaches his problem from the other side. Conceding the existence of personal immortality, he vindicates the uncertainty on the subject that is man's lot here. This vindication is carried on in an internal debate, which Browning endeavours to make as objective as possible in order that its result shall not be impeachable as the offspring of sentiment, the easy creation of wishes. Expressed in a more argumentative form, the substance of what 'Reason' says is that of *A Death in the Desert*, *Pisgah-Sights, II.*, and *Fears and Scruples*. It proves the value of ignorance in developing fortitude which comes of faith, morality which comes of volition, activity which comes of responsibility, and self-reliance which comes of the absence of authority.

La Saisiaz suffers from the personal directness which Browning disavows. The poem is so ratiocinative, that it needs characterisation to raise it generally to the imaginative level. The serpentining trochaics add to the strain on the attention, and what with the impetuous leaps, and only half expressed links, of its thought, it is one of Browning's hardest works.

The Two Poets of Croisic is enclosed between two exquisite lyrics. The one love of the personal life is the subject of the first (called *Appearances* in the *Selections*). The second (called *A Tale* in the *Selections*), is a story concerning a poet and his lyre. It brims over with playful tenderness, and tears—we need not ask for whom—are in the voice that tells us how once in the poet's life, the

> "string that made
> 'Love' sound soft was snapt in twain."

The Two Poets of Croisic unearths two personages, one of the sixteenth century, the other of the eighteenth. Each made a rocket-like ascent in Paris, fizzed awhile, and descended like rocket-sticks. Browning describes himself as sitting over a ship-wood fire, and telling what his fancy sees therein. He conjures up the bleak Breton fishing-village, Croisic, with its memoirs of Druidical savagery. His first Croisickese poet is René Gentilhomme, Condé's page, and a poetaster to whom came one hour of afflatus, or, as he and his world believed, of direct revelation. He prophesied the unhoped-for birth of Louis XIII. Afterwards, he wrote no more, a wise abstinence that gives him a title to respect in Browning's eyes. Stanzas lix.-lxvi. recall Browning's conception in *An Epistle* of the after-life of the raised Lazarus. Browning's second 'poet,' for whom a yellow-green flamelet does duty, is he whose history suggested Piron's *Métromanie*. Desforges-Maillard, stimulated by the earlier Croisickese example, determined to achieve greatness too. He forwarded his verses to *Le Mercure de France* to be contemptuously refused admission into its pages. While he fumed under the editor, La Roque's, treatment, his shrewder sister hit on a plan of redress. Copying out her brother's

effusions, and forwarding them with a girlish entreaty
and under a feminine pen-name, she not only subdued
La Roque, and presently had him at her feet in a love-
letter, but also extracted homage from Voltaire, and
adulation from literary Paris. The Breton Sappho,
as they called her, doubtless enjoyed the continuance
of her joke, but the conceit of Desforges-Maillard
could not long endure the vicarious reputation. He
journeyed to Paris and stormed the editor. La
Roque hid his discomfiture, and, to spite Voltaire, to
whom he, being a man of letters, owed a grudge, he
passed him on the hoax. A glance was sufficient to
explain the situation to Voltaire, and Desforges-
Maillard was speedily returned—empty—to Brittany.
The following extract from Voltaire's correspondence
amusingly connects the poem with literary history:
"L'aventure de la Malcrais-Maillard est assez plais-
ante. Elle prouve au moins que nous sommes très-
galants; car quand Maillard nous écrivait, nous ne
lisions pas ses vers; quand Mdlle de la Vigne nous
écrivit, nous lui fîmes des déclarations."

At the end of his story, Browning turns to his
auditor and gives her a test for judging poets. That
poet, he says, who leads the happiest life is the
greatest, because a poet necessarily feels, *i.e.* suffers,
more than others, and if he can but yoke his feelings
to his chariot, instead of being torn to pieces by them,
he proves his pre-eminence.

Dramatic Idyls, *First Series*, 1879, (Vol. XV.),
show the poet of unexpectedness at the top of

his bent. Twists, surprises, abrupt turns which seem, though they are not actually, changes of idea, are ingredients in every poem. In *Dramatic Idyls*, Browning collects a number of traditions and legends of sensational action. But where others see the act, Browning sees the motive, and so, in his accustomed way, he gives the action as from within, identifying himself with the doer. Accordingly, these dramatic idyls illustrate character in action, not action by and for itself. All the poems depict crises of character, or those determining moments of life on the significance of which Browning never tires of dwelling. The circumstances of the stories are tragic, the impression left by many of them painful and sad, for whereas former moral struggles as realised by Browning have, as a rule, resulted in victory for the soul, the stories of rare, yet thinkable trials in *Martin Relph*, *Iva̍n Iva̍novitch*, and *Clive*, with their dread moral abysses, solely evoke from the depths of us the trembling prayer, Lead *us* not into such temptation. Browning's own reconcilement with much that is repellent, fierce, and criminal in the subjects of his poems is to be found in the concluding lines of *Halbert and Hob*. A spiritual unknown quantity, the 'reason out of nature,' is never far from Browning's image of life, and we see how it operates in his presentment even of such characters as Halbert, Hob, and the Bratts'.

Martin Relph records an old man's self-imposed penance of annually standing just where he succumbed to temptation, and telling the surrounding crowd how, when he was young, he played coward, and, as he darkly knows, murderer. A girl, suspected of dealing with the Pretender's friends, was to be shot, by military law. Martin Relph alone saw a man hurrying with the reprieve, but made no sign, and a double death ensued—the girl's by the muskets, her hastening lover's by the despair of hearing them fired. Was Martin Relph's muteness due to cowardice or to something worse — jealous envy? Browning's intense vividness, and active sympathy with his characters, guilty or innocent, coarse or subtle, come out strongly in Martin Relph's lamentable confession. All the dramatist is in that change of tense from "was" to "am" as the anguished old man revives the searing scene that constitutes his past. The sympathy the poem excites is with the lover, Vincent Parkes. But the maddening hindrances he met in bringing the pardon, the despairing ignorance of the girl as to the cause of his non-arrival, and the climax of his being too late and thereat falling dead, are rendered all the more tragic through being ever afterwards Martin Relph's instruments of self-torture.

Pheidippides has for motto the Greek salutation that was born of Marathon day, "Rejoice, we conquer!" The poem is a beautiful adaptation from the story of the runner, Pheidippides, who in forty-eight hours accomplished the one hundred and fifty miles between Athens and Sparta, to ask help against the invading Persians. The request was virtually refused by the malicious Spartans. Returning, Pheidippides met Pan, who gave him a sprig of marathrus for a pledge of his aid, but juggled, as gods will, with his personal hopes. The story stands out with something of the joyful pride of a nobly proportioned Greek statue among its Gothic associates, between the sobbing passion of Martin Relph, and the Northern gloom of the next poem.

Halbert and Hob treats of that phonograph-like conservation of force, heredity, which can bottle up, for a generation or more, some climax of character, or rather some efflorescence of it in action, and then discharge it, seemingly oblivious of the fact that the particular exponent of the hereditary trait is a fresh person. There is just enough difference between Hob's behaviour and what Halbert recalls as his to make the story as true to the variety as to the similarity between related individuals. Here, indeed, the trait deepens by transmission. The incident of the poem is hideous till we get that gleam in the gloom, that true light from Browning's soul into the dark places of his mind, expressed in the close. Browning can dissociate his imagination from the vision of beauty, and ponder heredity with any Northerner, but he is an optimist. Yet he is rarely as pathetic as in the lines,

"'At his cursing and swearing!' the youngsters cried: but the elders thought 'In prayer.'
A boy threw stones: he picked them up and stored them in his vest."

At the same time, Hob's violence has to be punished, and idiocy, consequent on the moral revolution, comes upon him.

Ivàn Ivànovitch embodies the Russian folk-lore tale of the wretched woman in the sledge who saved herself from the wolves at the price of her children's lives. Characteristically, and in this case not shrinking from the utmost frightful realism, Browning speaks as the woman herself. Her description of the unnatural light, half snowy, half moony, in the pine-forest, the horrible attacks of the wild beasts, and her own agony of physical fear are almost unbearably exciting. Afterwards comes the judgment, when Ivàn Ivànovitch strikes off the head of the woman who could so surrender her children. And yet this thrilling tale, letting us into the sophistries, the supreme weakness of the woman, does not terminate the poem. Where any other teller would stop, Browning has still much to say. He has not only to present Ivàn Ivànovitch's execution of the unmotherly mother, but to give the judgment articulateness through the aged priest—Innocent XII. in another dress. We must feel for the woman in her terrible trial, but Browning heightens her guilt by representing her as afterwards able to congratulate herself on her escape, and to look forward to pleasant years, instead of being overwhelmed with remorse, wakened as it were from a hideous nightmare of her own selfishness. That callous vileness is the justification of the carpenter's deed. The contrasts and strong unity in Iván's character are extremely dramatic. The part of the poem we could least readily spare is the final paragraph, where the vindicator of the primal justice kneels building the model Kremlin for his own children.

Tray is a curious and effective little poem, not the less so on account of the obvious anachronism between the Bard who tells his tale to a kind of François Ier and the eighteenpenny vivisection in the tale itself. Browning's short pieces are condensed dramas, and the multiplicity of ideas even in the shortest is strikingly exemplified here. The characteristic after-gust which we find in each poem in this collection is here the humans' complacent superiority over the dog against whom they plan their cold-blooded treachery while he gave them his spontaneous generosity.

Ned Bratts is founded on 'The Story of old *Tod*' in Bunyan's *Life and Death of Mr. Badman.* To compare the poem with the original is to deepen one's sense of Browning's imagination. *Ned Bratts* is a feat of execution peculiar even in Browning, and resembling Hogarth more than any other Englishman. The fiery heat, fittest temperature for the hysterics of revivalism with its coarse effects on brutalised people, is wonderfully realised. The 'cause out of nature,' here *The Pilgrim's Progress*, is, however, according to Browning, not to be reasoned away by a midsummer madness explanation. This is the only time a poet has approached the problem of conversions. As given in *Ned Bratts*, the selflessness of Bunyan and the selfishness of his doctrine when crystallised by the gross people to whom it appealed as giving them hold of the highest card form a chapter in theological criticism.

Second Series, 1880. The proem suggests what most of the 'Dramatic Idyls' illustrate, the unaccountability, according to scientific *data*, of 'man's soul.' Our test-tubes and plummets cannot resolve, cannot dive into human motive. There is always that to count on which Browning describes as something 'out of nature,' the finger of God, the assertion of the individual and freedom of his will.

Echetlos (The Holder of the Ploughshare) is a memory from Marathon, a poem that goes hand in hand with *Pheidippides*.

Clive gives a story, referred to in Macaulay's Essay, of the 'great unhappy' Indian hero. Clive is described as telling an old friend when, of all his days of peril and bravery, he felt most fear. It was when, still a lad, he failed to shoot a bully whom he had detected cheating at cards. Clive's pistol missed, and he stood to be shot. His steadiness unnerved the cheat, who, confessing his disgrace, fled the company. These eleven Clive bound over to silence, with a stern word on their behaviour in the proceeding. So far the story is obvious. Browning's sign-manual upon it is still to come. . . . It was not death Clive feared when the pistol fronted his brow. What he dreaded was reprieve, a discreet forgiveness that would have left him two alternatives, disgrace or suicide. Here his interlocutor interposes an orthodox objection—it needs more courage to disobey God's canon against self-slaughter than to bear reputed disgrace. Now comes the effectiveness of the Browning interpolation. A week after the conversation, Clive destroyed himself. His last words were, 'fearfully courageous!' So had the opium-drugged man designated what he did in a fit of depression, so had he clung to a possible interpretation of his friend's words as some desperate excuse.

Muléykeh is a touching story of an Arab's pride in his steed. It comes refreshingly after the melancholy of *Clive*. The pathos of *Muléykeh* is bearable.

Pietro of Abano reads drearily after these vivid and warm-blooded poems. The 'lilt' is of course extremely clever and well-suited to the quasi-comic treatment. Pietro of Abano (a suburb of Padua) was a sort of inferior Paracelsus of the thirteenth century, of whom it is recorded that he was prohibited the drinking of milk. Browning takes this milk as parabolic, or at least suggestive, of the human kindness which a misunderstood benefactor of mankind has to forego. One night, the persecuted philosopher was accosted by a Greek who offered him gratitude and love if he would endow him with his powerful secrets. Pietro seems to comply, muttering the first half of a *Benedicite* as a charm. The self-seeking Greek begins by applying the secret of

Good the fruit of Evil to the furtherance of his own schemes for obtaining wealth from his fellows. The method succeeds. In a year's time, Pietro calls upon the Greek for his payment. But the Greek prefers to postpone it till Pietro has endowed him with power to subjugate men. Power becomes his, and, at the height of his success, Pietro again asks for gratitude. This is again deferred, on the plea that the Greek must first touch the top of the ladder, and wield power over souls as well as bodies. His request is granted and he is Pope. Pietro comes again, and is about to be unceremoniously ousted, when he utters the latter half of the *Benedicite*. The spell is broken, and the Greek finds that Pietro only gave him an instant's dream of greatness, to test the sincerity of his promised gratitude. Pietro's would-be disciple is dismissed, Browning telling him that magic is unnecessary to one so well able to rule the masses by 'cleverness uncurbed by conscience.' The conclusion is cynical, but Browning regards his version of Abano's legend [1] as a mere vagary, a throw of 'sportive fancy-dice.'

Doctor —— renders the Talmudic tradition of Satan married to a virago who is more than his match. The touch of humour in Satan's medical son refusing the princess and her dowry on account of his father's unfortunate matrimonial experience is Browning's after-gust to the story.

Pan and Luna is in some respects one of Brown-

---

[1] Cp. Grimms' *The Fisherman and his Wife*.

ing's most perfect gems. Keats could not have lingered more lovingly about the Girl-moon's orbed loveliness. Browning averts Virgil's somewhat equivocal conclusion of the myth by acknowledging himself gratefully content to rest on the five consummate ideas,

'Arcadia, night, a cloud, Pan, and the moon!'

The epilogue to *Dramatic Idyls*, with its contrasted presentments of poet - nature, presentments which after all are probably in Browning's eyes but the inevitable two sides of a shield, recalls the *Epilogue* to *Pacchiarotto*.

Jocoseria, 1883 (Vol. XV.), is a volume of miscellaneous poems, made up of Browning's twin moods, gravity and jest. The *Joco-Seria* of Melander (16—)[1] suggested the title. Browning's personality is strong in *Jocoseria*, on his *capriccioso* side, as in *Solomon and Balkis*, and on the side of his creed, as in the last utterance of Jochanan Hakkadosh. Individuality, not poetical beauty, characterises the book, though it contains a leaven of imaginative exaltation in *Ixion* and *Cristina and Monaldeschi*.

The prelude, 'Wanting is—what?' expresses the vivifying, transmuting power of love in a life.

Donald is a striking but improbable story with a somewhat unfair application. A short introduction

[1] A reference was made in the *Notes* on *Paracelsus* to this jestbook, in which, too, a version of the story immortalised in *The Pied Piper* appears under the title of *De Diabolo horrenda historia*.

(time, Long Vacation; place, a Highland Bothie), ushers in the story, as told, in another bothie, by the odious protagonist. 'Donald' met a stag on a narrow way, above a precipice, where they could neither turn nor pass each other. The man lay down, and the stag, with responsive intelligence, was daintily stepping over him, when Donald, without a vestige of a sense of honour, stabbed him. They rolled together down the ravine, and Donald had to repent his deed for the rest of his life. Browning tells the tale as a retort to those who maintain that Sport educes manly virtues. He calls the wretched ingrate, 'sportsman first, man after.' As a matter of fact, the treacherous brutality was not sport any more than the animal's action was nature, and Donald's meanness would be as abhorrent to honest sportsmen as to Browning himself.

Solomon and Balkis is an extravaganza of sound and sense. Solomon and the Queen of Sheba hold high converse on the ivory throne, till the lady, jerking the hand of the King, brings into sight 'the truth-compelling Name' on the royal ring. It then comes out that Solomon's boasted delight in the companionship of wise men is largely tinctured with vanity and love of flattery, and that Balkis is not to be taken literally when she professes a disinterested eagerness for the companionship of the simply good. She is a frivolous, but fascinating 'cat,' but Solomon is the very Solomon of history.

Cristina and Monaldeschi, though it may be justly accused of obscurity, resembles in dramatic fervency the grand poems of *Men and Women*. Cristina, 'King' of Sweden, the only child of Gustavus Adolphus, abdicated after four years' rule. She was extraordinarily brilliant, but restless and fickle. Her voice and bearing were manly, and she occasionally assumed masculine garb. Marchese Monaldeschi, her Secretary, disgracefully divulged her secrets, and his violent execution was at least as much in punishment for political treachery as for waning personal devotion. Louis XIV. had assigned Cristina the palace of Fontainebleau for a residence, and there, on November 1st, 1657, she had Monaldeschi killed in the Gallery of Stags. Monaldeschi, coward as well as traitor, wore beneath his clothes a shirt of mail, which prolonged his death. An hour's previous conversation between him and Cristina actually took place, she pacing the gallery, while he, kneeling and prostrating himself, implored her to spare his life. Monaldeschi was buried in the church of Avon, a neighbouring village.

Mary Wollstonecraft and Fuseli is a lonely woman's cry for love. The poem represents a strong, but baffled nature, and so far reflects the general impression received from Mary's life. Whether Browning, following Fuseli's biographer, is not unjust to her in this particular episode of her career, does not, in the poet's case, very much matter. The poem rests on its truth to nature, not to Mary Wollstonecraft.

Adam, Lilith, and Eve is excellent fooling, where, like Shakspere's, the serious lies near the jocular. Eve confesses to her husband that her superficial disdain of him before they were married would at any moment have melted at his kiss. Lilith makes a more sinister avowal, viz. that she only married Adam because a better man did not turn up. With practical wisdom, Adam winks at the confessions of both his dames.

Ixion is Browning's word on future punishment. The uses of torment are over when the tormented has learned from it the error of his past. Injustice, not justice, schemes eternal expiation for crimes committed against itself by short-lived ignorance and weakness. Ixion can whirl on his agonising wheel, yet rejoice in his moral superiority. He rises 'past Zeus to the Potency o'er him.' The sweat, blood, and tears that fly off from the wheel make a rainbow of hope. Prometheus-like, Ixion has wrung from his suffering a gift for men—the certainty that Unreason and Injustice cannot be supreme, that the tyrannous 'Zeus' is less than God, because worse than man. The man-made Zeus who first tempts, then tortures eternally, has no real existence. Browning's denial of the reality of a 'Zeus' separates, in the latter part of the poem, from Ixion's protest against the injustice of his tyrant.

Jochanan Hakkadosh is introduced as a set-off to *Doctor* —— of the *Dramatic Idyls*. It follows the favourite direction of Browning's mind, about this period, towards Oriental stories and surroundings. *Jochanan Hakkadosh* is professedly derived (see *Note* at end) from a Rabbinical work, called *A Collection of many Lies.* Such a title sufficiently proves itself 'mere fun and invention.' The Jewish saint (*Hakkadosh-Saint*) lies dying, surrounded by sorrowing disciples. They beg a last word which shall concentrate the stored experience of the Rabbi's nine and seventy years. Jochanan's reply amounts to an avowal that his life has proved vain, ineffectual, and vexing to his spirit, because his youth did not know, his age could not do. He bids his scholars farewell, but they cannot bear to part with him without having learned more, so they bethink them of a means, known to Talmudists, whereby Jochanan's life can be prolonged a little. This may be effected by the gifts of short periods from the lives of other people, which can be grafted on the dying man. An eager competition to give ensues. Four persons only are chosen, a lover, a warrior, a poet, and a statesman. Each contributes three months, and, at the end of each period, Tsaddik, Jochanan's foremost disciple, comes to his master to gather his words of wisdom. These arrange themselves into comments on the special form of life Jochanan has last imbibed. Remembering that the four fractions of lives were all taken from the young, we are prepared for their artificial and discordant effect upon the octogenarian. First comes the word on love. Worship and idealism of the beloved object, enthusiasm for her charms and qualities are graces proper to a young man, but impossible to the aged experience of Jochanan. Feeling and his reason being irreconcilable, 'love' appears bitterness and vanity. Similar incongruity between the outlook of youth and age is apparent in Jochanan's word on war. The sage knows that self-sacrifice can be practised at less cost than by wholesale murder. He knows, too, that the end striven for rarely justifies— or is worth — the strife. Men seldom attain by violence what they might not as well have waited for. Next as to poetry. Its materials are hope and the future, but as Jochanan has only the petrified past to gaze upon, his view of poetry is all disillusionment. Statecraft lastly comes in for its share of pessimistic criticism. The statist has to legislate for the mindless masses who obstruct, not for the cultured few who would encourage his schemes. Tsaddik, who had hoped to compile a work on *The Science of Man's Life* from Jochanan's utterances, feels that this gospel of disillusionment will be of no use to any body. Sorrowfully, he leaves Jochanan for dead. Three months elapse, and the faithful visit the cave where their master's body lies. To their astonishment, they find Jochanan still living and supremely happy. A new light has broken in upon him. He calls it 'ignorance confirmed by knowledge.' He now sees life from heaven's standpoint, acquiesces in the ignorance and failures of mortals, and knows that all is well. Life, he declares, is a wine-press, whose yield is known only in the next state. Yet Jochanan, breathing his last, feels he cannot impart his beautiful secret, for it is incomprehensible to men. Of this fact the zealous Tsaddik, in his misapprehension of what Jochanan meant by 'the secret,' gives ample corroboration.

Jochanan Hakkadosh is followed by three jocular Sonnets, delicious exaggerations on the subject of Og's hugeness. These are the first sonnets Browning published, and the only ones at present included in his *Works*. The idea in *Jochanan* is of the finite striving to reach the infinite, and in the sonnets the idea of unattainable distance and dimension is bandied about in pure merriment.

Never the Time and the Place expresses love's conquest over distrust. In the prelude, Browning spoke of love as completing all that lacks without it, and here he speaks of it as atoning for all other incompleteness.

Pambo is an *Envoy* in which Browning amusingly compares himself to a student who spent much time trying to master the verse, "I will take heed to my ways that I sin not with my tongue." Pambo is to be met with in Wanley's *Wonders of the Little World* among illustrations 'Of the Veracity of some Persons, their great Love to Truth.' Browning knows that the 'darkling' character of his muse is the very rock of offence with his critics.

Ferishtah's Fancies, 1884 (Vol. XVI.), deals with twelve subjects of religious thought. These are put in quaint Persian guise and in the form of parables and discussions, sprinkled with lines of dry humour. A beautiful lyric follows each 'Fancy,' to re-incarnate its spirit, or rather to give an analogy to

it, chiefly from the experience of a pair of English
lovers. To preface his work, Browning quotes from
the speech of Lear's that he so illumined in *Halbert
and Hob* by his comment. This time, the apt quotation
signifies what the author of *Pauline*, *At the " Mermaid,"*
and *House* could hardly be expected to declare openly,
viz. that the 'garments' are 'Ferishtah's,' but the
speculations are the speculations of Browning. Never
before, indeed, has a poet expressed so specifically and
categorically as in *Ferishtah's Fancies* his attitude
towards the moot points of theistic influence. It is not
in Browning's fearless, truth-loving nature to shrink
from the responsibilities of his belief—or rather his
surmise, for the fervent faith of *Abt Vogler* is
chastened at this later period by a deeper conviction
of the unthinkable nature of God.

Prologue is a whimsical allegory of the scheme of
the poems. They are to combine three 'flavours':—
the illustration of Ferishtah's lesson, which is the
plain toasted bread—'sense'; the lesson itself, which
is the sage-leaf—'sight'; and the lyrical variation on
the theme, which is the ortolan—'song.'

The Eagle narrates Ferishtah's call to dervish-hood.
By a miracle and a dream, he learns that God works
through human means, and that whoever can, must
support himself and afterwards support the weak.

The lyric enshrines a similar idea. Love is not
to consist in the selfish isolation of two lives. Freely
the lovers have received, freely let them give.

The Melon-Seller resembles the ancient story of the

philosophic slave who accepted the bitter gourd. All God's gifts are of grace, 'the less deserved, the more divine.' His stripes alone are 'just' (see Job ii. 10).

In the lyric, the lover prays his love not to retract an unwonted harshness. If she is for strict justice, none of all her kindness will remain his.

Shah Abbas deals with the difficulties of historico-religious belief. An eager desire to believe a story counts for more than an intellectual assent to its truth which neither touches the emotions nor influences the life. Love, even if it cannot justify itself, is dearer to God than a cold credence.

In darkness, every piece of furniture is a stumbling-block, but when once the lamp is lit, no obstacles obstruct the way. Love resembles that lamp.

The Family treats of the value of prayer. 'If God is wise, good, and mighty, why pray to Him, as though man knew more than He?' To this familiar objection, Ferishtah replies, 'Man obeys the heart's instinct in praying. If he shared God's omniscience, he would not pray, but human as he is, he does best to act as humanity urges. Let him pray according to ignorance, and God will answer according to Knowledge.'

The lover is content to love as a mere man. Therefore he will not pretend he looks for perfections which, as man, he could not appreciate.

The Sun approaches the Incarnation from the philosophical side. Ferishtah claims personality for the Deity because he himself possesses it. Yet purpose and will, the elements of personality, are so incompatible with omnipotence that he can but confess the God that man creates in his own image utterly incomprehensible. Such is the enigma. May not its solution lie in a 'rumour' there is that

> "God once assumed on earth a human shape"?

The beginning of the poem recalls *An Epistle*, and the conclusion, *A Death in the Desert*.

The lyric gives a familiar illustration of a kinship which might well appear as inconceivable as that between flesh and fire, man and God, viz. the kinship between fire and flint.

Mihrab Shah contains Browning's reply to the immemorial problem of the existence of suffering. 'Pain is the bond of sympathy between man and man.' The dialogue in this poem is particularly vigorous and vivacious, yet *Mihrab Shah* is somewhat disappointing. We cannot feel that Ferishtah's hardy optimism really helps to lighten the burden of the mystery.

The idea is more touchingly expressed in the lyric.

A Camel-Driver, like *Ixion*, discusses the dogma of eternal punishment. 'Man's punishments of man have but one motive—to deter the offender from offending again or the by-standers from following his example. After death, and with God, all is different. But let none envy him who escapes man's punishment.' Browning is assured that tardy knowledge is Hell's severest penalty. "Forgiveness? rather grant forgetfulness!" The thought of the unconditioned relation between the individual and God is again strong, and the lines,

> "Reason aims to raise
> Some makeshift scaffold-vantage midway, whence
> Man dares, for life's brief moment, peer,"

sum up most of the teaching of the entire volume, particularly that of *The Sun* and *A Bean-Stripe*.

The lyric dwells on the faultiness of human judgments.

Two Camels condemns that self-regarding mortification of the flesh which unfits a man for doing God's work efficiently. God looks to the end for the multiplication of the talents, and it is man's wisdom to adopt the best means thereto. Again, how is an ascetic to contribute conscientiously to the joy of others? No; God who sends joy and the capacity for joy may be trusted for the wisdom of His gifts.

Heaven itself may be an eternisation of life's moments of bliss.

Cherries teaches us not to think gratitude to God is to be reserved for great mercies. Little blessings best suit our little lives. Cherries please the palate of him to whom the reason why various planets exist is incomprehensible. God's omnipotence is even more displayed in His considering our everyday requirements than in His creating the remote greatness of Jupiter.[1] Man, in return, is to act, however small his action be. Neither is he to be downcast

[1] Cp. *Giuseppe Caponsacchi*, ll. 2090-2096.

by the mixture of motives in his offering. The chief matter is to offer something.

The lyric repeats Ferishtah's last sentiment.

Plot-Culture, like *Two Camels*, justifies sense and its gratification. God has regard to the harvest, not to the year's daily processes towards it.

The particularly lyrical lyric restates the claims of sense.

A Pillar at Sebzevar demonstrates the worthlessness of knowledge as an end in itself, and the value of love. Knowledge is relative, but love is absolute. Ferishtah counsels his disciple to take so much truth as God has vouchsafed for his individual needs, and love and live by it, instead of investigating it and turning on it the dubious lenses of his 'knowledge.'

Silence may express admiration more eloquently than volubility.

A Bean-Stripe: also, Apple-Eating crowns Ferishtah's optimism. The sublimated spiritual egoism, or self-centralisation, of *Rabbi Ben Ezra* is the basis of the argument, yet while Browning herein emphasises afresh the declaration that his verdict on life is merely the result of individual experience, he goes on to express disbelief, not only in practical pessimism, but in any life being without compensation in some shape. He derives his cheerful yet sober view from the progress or 'motion' of life and the growth which he detects to be the soul's law. Blacks and whites ranged alternately and whirled rapidly show neither blackness nor whiteness but an amalgam of both. So, thanks to life's spiritual progression, happiness is saddened and sorrow brightened. When Ferishtah's scholar quarrels with this thesis for its want of absoluteness, Ferishtah defends it by demonstrating how unimaginable is all absolute truth. He instances (as previously in *The Sun*, to which he refers) our necessarily provisional concepts of God. At best, we can only know "what seems." To the objection that there may well seem to be no God but mindless force, Ferishtah replies that man's mind would be negatived by God's mindlessness. Man's instinct of gratitude is a presumption in favour of the existence of a being to whom he owes gratitude. It is next urged that the heroes of our race are fitter objects of gratitude than an unknown God. 'What, thank myself?' replies Ferishtah, 'for half the value of these benefactors' greatness lies in my perception of it. No, He who gave me the perception which suggests gratitude is the Recipient of my thanks.'

The lyric supposes one of these heroic men, a poet masked as 'Ferishtah,' disclaiming the worship a Comtist might offer him. The poet is answerable to God, not men.

Epilogue is touched with a reaction against the cheerfulness of *A Bean-Stripe*, the existence of which 'tremor' (see p. 77) the philosophy therein expressed faithfully acknowledged. What if, after all, the happy circumstances of the individual illusively paint the general life as worth living? Browning does not answer the question, but we feel the chill mood to be only momentary, and the last word, as well as the first, of *Ferishtah's Fancies* to be

> " 'Take what is, trust what may be!'
> That's Life's true lesson."

Parleyings with Certain People of Importance in their Day, 1887 (Vol. XVI.), is Browning's penultimate volume, and, in conjunction with *Asolando*, the last of his works, it not merely closes, but completes with a full carillon the range of music in our poet's belfry. Echoes and repeats of almost all the varied harmonies that have ever been there sound in *Parleyings*, not excepting certain bells that have scarcely been stirred since *Paracelsus* and *Sordello*, though Browning's distinctively lyrical note is reserved to ring out clear and sweet in *Asolando*. It is true that occasionally in the *Parleyings*, as in *Mandeville* and *Avison*, the bells are muffled in the harshness of argument and the oft-told tale of optimism to which the years since *The Ring and the Book* have inured us. What is the connecting link of these seven colloquies, their *Prologue*, and their *Epilogue*? It seems to be a sense of the multiformity of life, a sense which ever widening experience would only accentuate, and to which Browning's dramatic imagination and increasing acquiescence in the fact of man's spiritual darkness converge. A conviction that in the world evil cannot be dissociated from good, and a confession of ultimate ignorance united to an unconquerable determination to exercise that provisional knowledge which leads human existence to the highest expression of itself in thought and deed run through each 'parleying' on art and life. Characteristically, the brilliant book opens with Apollo, the god or soul of poetry, and closes with Fust, the printer, who ministers to literature as Browning believes body ministers to soul. The poetic glory, however, which Browning puts into the gamut between Fust and Apollo, and not the familiar views, is the principal fact about the book.

The serio-grotesque Introduction is circumstantially a Prologue in Hell to *Alkestis*, and really a summary of Browning's silver-lined-cloud philosophy of life. Browning purposely reduces the Fates to garrulous crones, far beneath Shakspere's 'weird sisters.' Sober, they deny life to be worth living; besotted, they pronounce it so well worth living that its triumph is absolute and unquestionable. It needs an earthquake to strike the mean, and convince these blind weavers, who were human for the nonce, that their shuttles

"Weave living, not life sole and whole: as age—youth,
So death completes living, shows life in its truth."

In other words, no human solution of life may conceit itself as final. At best, it is a crutch, with the uses and tacit assumption of one.

With Bernard de Mandeville is the first 'parleying.' Browning, with his love of paradox and belief in the inextricableness of good from evil, naturally turns his attention to the half forgotten fabulist of *The Grumbling Hive* (1705). Yet the cynical, materialistic doctor, whose views coincide with all that Browning's philosophy disavows, is a curious supporter of a piece of transcendentalism, though this felt discrepancy does not affect the purpose of Browning's poem. The real 'parleying' is not with Mandeville, but with another, one who was 'more of a dynamic than a didactic force,' and the invocation of Mandeville's argumentative aid does not necessarily involve any thing beyond the train of ideas which the alternative title of *The Bees* (viz. *Private Vices Public Benefits*), freely interpreted, suggests to Browning.

With Daniel Bartoli does not even take its text from the invoked Jesuit writer. It is 'a fancy-freak by contrast born of' his *long-winded stories, which might be read, were they not so ruinously full of all manner of superstitions.* "Saint me no saints!" Browning virtually says to the ingenious Bartoli, "I will draw you a woman who outsaints them." Then follows a story which in treatment resembles Browning's *The Glove*.

With Christopher Smart contains deeper harmonies. Smart's *Song to David* is the hint on which Browning writes, and he deals with the relation between the one perfect product, the 'single speech' which some men achieve and the mediocre residue of their lifework. The illustration of the jewel-like chapel amid the commonplaceness of the huge house, by which Browning introduces his subject, is a never-to-be-forgotten treasure of imaginative criticism. Section ix. is, as Browning acknowledges, an explanation of which Smart could never have thought. Its idea is that economy exists in poetic production, that the vitalising, Adamic work of naming, which is the poet's supreme gift to the world, is a gift conditional on the use to which the world puts it. Only so much as can, or will, be utilised does the wise poet disburse. His treasures are, like God's revelation, sparingly given, and only on the understanding that they prick men on to advance.

With George Bubb Dodington is a caustic mock-reproof to a knavish fool, in this case the most crawling politician of Walpole's time. The Sludge-like course ironically recommended to him, which he was not artful enough to take, resembles that already outlined in the third stage of the Greek in *Pietro of Abano*. 'Inscrutableness is statecraft's highest card, and it takes more than ordinary guile to rule the masses who are already versed in all the commoner strategies of selfishness.'

With Francis Furini primarily upholds the right of high Art to depict the nude. Baldinucci (of *Privilege of Burial* memory!), in his biography of the painter-priest, Furini, tells the well-known story of how, on his death-bed, the artist sought to destroy his pictures of undraped womanhood.

"Nay, *that*, Furini, never I at least
Mean to believe!"

begins Browning, whose faculty for scorn and indignation is more directly shown here than in any other poem. His plea for the nude in Art is one with his reverence for God's best handiwork. An artist, he goes on to say, who would express spirit truthfully can only do so by painting flesh truthfully, since the whole body expresses the soul, which, bodiless, would be inexpressive. The more philosophical parts of the poem are linked to the rest by the relation between the study of the human form and the basis of 'Furini's' philosophy, self-consciousness. The shade of the 'painter-theologian' asserts that this self-consciousness, or this fact of soul, is approached and known by studying the revealer and medium of soul, body. The design and beneficence of which he becomes more deeply aware the closer he studies lead him on to recognise the 'out'-soul, God. Thus is life turned cosmos by 'Furini,' who dares the evolutionists to prove it on their showing any thing but chaos. The poem ends with a lovely passage which is not exactly comparable with any other in Browning. It is as quiet and simple as it is great.

With Gerard de Lairesse, the grandest and most significant of the 'parleyings,' addresses itself to the Dutch painter and writer on Art who in his blind age went about fancying Holland peopled with gods and goddesses. Browning challenges fantasy to match fact, and then enters the lists in the cause of reality against de Lairesse, who may reasonably be considered a champion of dreams. Browning, who in many respects lags behind 'latest developments,' here heads the van of progress and gives the finest poetic expression it has yet received to the essentially modern passion for nature unendowed with any factitious attributes. The poem, every word of which is poetry, comes from the old, hopeful poet as an inspiring cry of 'forward.'

With Charles Avison reads like a continuation of the thoughts on music in *Fifine at the Fair*. Avison was an eighteenth century composer, of whom, as of de Lairesse, Browning speaks as an early friend. We may probably accept as a certainty that most of the old-world characters whose names are borrowed for these 'parleyings' belong to memories of the poet's boyish reading. Browning evidently shares in the touching instinct of life's decline to return to its earliest associations. Every art, says Browning, strives to arrest the evanescence of feeling, to 'shoot liquidity into a mould,' and none fails like music, feeling's most direct language, because no other art is so susceptible of change and superannuation. Yet the truths which music strives to register are undying. Each composer is good, and best in that he represents a link in music's chain, not an independent ring, final and complete for ever. These ideas about music, its pathos and its glory, ruled *Abt Vogler*, only there they were transmuted into sensation, while here they are merely thought.

Fust and his Friends is a playful glimpse at the infancy of printing. Besides this, it is, more implicitly, a comment, in the spirit of the entire volume, on the fleeting nature of our knowledge, its liability to abuse, and withal its capacity of begetting new knowledge, which shall be in advance of it, just as Luther was in advance of Huss.

Asolando: Fancies and Facts, 1890, is invested with a pathetic interest from the circumstances of its publication. It was published on the day on which Browning died, and his last words, "how gratifying!" were in acknowledgment of the telegraphed news of its anticipatory welcome. Thus the book has come to have a sacredness, a personal association of memory which, at all events at present, render an impartial appreciation of it almost impossible. One prefers to dwell upon its unmistakable gems, such as *Poetics* and *Summum Bonum*, rather than criticise its tenuous reveries and tales wherein we catch little more than the echo of more vigorous achievement. It is clear that the general date of 1889 cannot be assigned to each poem, though we cannot say how many may be referred to earlier periods of production. Some, as *Dubiety, Poetics, Inapprehensiveness, Development*, seem more specially sheafed than others by the binding threads of the *Prologue* and *Epilogue*, and these may probably be taken as the indubitable 'Asolani.' Their peculiar note is one which could only emanate from a poet who is reviewing life from its further end. It is that truth surpasses fiction as fact surpasses fancy, while, at the same time, that fiction, far from being worthless, is the sole ladder up to truth. Browning's readers remember in *Sordello* and *Pippa Passes* the introduction of Asolo, the small white city of the Trevisan, mountains behind and Lombard plain before, which, roughly speaking, lies, for the traveller, between Bassano and Vicenza. After Venice, Asolo was the first place in Italy that Browning visited (1838), and it is the last (1889) with which he is poetically associated. He was as faithful to his love for Asolo as he was to all his loves. And here, on the threshold of Browning's last work, we may reiterate what has been at all events held in solution by every page of these comments, viz. that Browning's 'genius' was the expressive side of his whole nature. The more we ponder what we learn from Browning's poetry, and then compare it with the little we need to learn of his life, the more we are struck by the unity of the impression which as a personality, compounded of genius and man, he makes upon us, lovable in foibles and weakness as in nobleness and strength.

Prologue is the lyric counterpart of *Gerard de Lairesse*. To a poet of Browning's sage, sweet temperament and development, years and 'disillusionment' bring, not despondency, but gladness at seeing truth drop the wraps that bound her.

Rosny, with its dramatic characterisation and abrupt, perhaps bewildering, plunge into the centre of the situation, belongs to the same class as *Cristina and Monaldeschi*. It is spoken by a woman, armed at all points against her unsuccessful rival, the 'Clara' addressed. Rosny is away in the war, but whether he returns safely or falls, Clara shall have no share in his victory or sacrifice, shall not even know that her rival can feel anything besides the calmness of perpetual superiority. There is something soulless and eerie about the speaker which is indeterminately heightened by the refrain of names.

Dubiety records an hour of mild, autumnal gladness. Whence and whereby did it come? Not on the wings of sleep or day-dream. It was a *memory* of love.

'Truth ever, truth only the excellent!'

Now is a poem of fourteen lines upon such a moment of love as eternalises time, or rather annihilates the conception of it.

Humility is the poet's lovely thought concerning the ungrudged crumbs which fall from the banquet of one who makes love rich.

Poetics is the name by which Browning designates the metaphors of lovers. 'Rose,' 'swan,' 'moon,' to these the adored one is compared, while all the time she surpasses them by being a beautiful human creature.

Summum Bonum ranks among the perfect short love-poems of the English language. The manliness and restraint of Browning are upon a poem the melody and words of which sound more like a lyric of Mr. Swinburne's. Let us bear in mind that this exquisite piece, as full of freshness as it is simple, was put forth by a poet of seventy-seven.

A Pearl, a Girl is hardly less delightful than *Summum Bonum*.

Speculative might well be a lyric from *Ferishtah's Fancies*. It is similar in idea to the conclusion of the one that follows *Two Camels*.

White Witchcraft dallies with the innocence of love and the playful mutual mockery in which tenderness can securely indulge.

Bad Dreams. I. is a remarkable instance of how much a great poet can condense into a couple of quatrains of the simplest words.

Bad Dreams. II. is a curious piece of delicately suggested horror. Its phantasmagoria recalls Tennyson's *Vision of Sin*. A lover sees in his dream the girl he worships involved in a grisly and bestial cult. He charges her with it, and she retorts upon him with a dream of her own, probably similar in origin, but ludicrously dispersive of his troubled sensations regarding her.

Bad Dreams. III. is a nightmare on the grand scale of upheaval and topsy-turveydom.

Bad Dreams. IV. records, in a particularly striking way, a man's bitter regret and remorse for the death of the girl who loved and was affianced to him. He had systematically snubbed her for her deficient mental culture, and chilled her heart by his cold scorn of her frivolous ways. Love had been disguised as blame and criticism. Now she is dead through his unkindness, and he would thankfully humble himself to the dust to have her alive and forgiving him.

Inapprehensiveness, somewhat in the spirit of the preceding poem, tells of a woman who is entirely absorbed in verifying a writer's observation on a weed, and utterly unconscious of the love for herself which is consuming her companion—

"Oh, fancies that might be, oh, facts that are!"

The worst of it is that her 'inapprehensive stare' freezes the expression of the man's love, so that he merely replies to her cultured remark with a similar one. We recall *Two in the Campagna* when we read *Inapprehensiveness*.

Which? paints subtle portraits in miniature. The Countess is willing to be Providence to a lover, provided he on his side refers solely to her for salvation. We are left to decide whether such an ideal of love, if genuine, is or is not an arrogant usurpation of God's prerogative.

The Cardinal and the Dog is of a class of story in frequent demand in a children's hour.

The Pope and the Net is one of those *bizarreries*, like the story of Judas and the fowl in *Juris Doctor Johannes-Baptista Bottinius*, for which Browning has a keen relish.

The Bean-Feast is in the cast of thought of *Ferishtah's Fancies*.

Muckle-Mouth Meg is a pleasant Border ballad.

Arcades Ambo censures vivisection, which it defines with animosity and dubs cowardice.

The Lady and the Painter effectively inveighs against

a conventionalism that approves a woman who wears the wings and breasts of murdered birds, and disapproves another who, as a model, suffers her beautiful form to be reproduced in marble or on canvas.

Ponte dell' Angelo, Venice, belongs to a group of poems Browning has written on traditions of places. Like the Greeks, he is partial to wiliness, especially when, as here, it is a saint who gets the better of the evil one.

Beatrice Signorini is a pretty tale of a Griselda who had the wit on a provocative occasion to turn Katharine and thereby rose immeasurably in her husband's estimation.

Flute Music, with an Accompaniment is a dialogue, the ideas of which are suggested by a flautist's playing heard through the ash-trees. A woman ridicules the poetic construction which a man puts upon the fluting. At last, he turns the tables upon her by affecting, at all events, to take her cynical words as descriptive and consequently condemnatory of her own ways with him. The poem is accurately described by its title, the precise meaning that may be put upon the words being subsidiary — an 'accompaniment' to their music.

"*Imperante Augusto natus est* ——" is a contemporary comment on the greatness and glories of Augustus. It gives the story of his annual donning of a beggar's garb in order to avert the jealousy of the divine element so dreaded by the Romans. The title and the allusion at the end of the poem refer to the so-called Messianic prophecy in one of the (forged) Sybilline books. The poem accentuates the prevailing Roman sentiment of the uncertainty of things and the nearness of supremacy to destruction.

Development is an interesting and delightful parable of Browning's philosophy of illusion and growth.

Rephan in a noble and imaginative manner expresses contentment with the limitations, difficulties, and ignorance in which mankind lives.

Reverie expresses Browning's belief that Love is the hidden name of Power. On earth, Power and Love appear dissociated, because on earth man is meant to grope his own way and attest the stuff of which he is made.

Epilogue is the last word spoken by Browning to the world. It is an epilogue not only to *Asolando* but to the whole of his life. Though it is not a poem that epitomises his genius, it is one that calls up a backward-glancing vision of the particular influence he has everywhere exercised over his readers. The *Epilogue* to *Asolando* at least reminds us of Browning's bracing, tonic effect upon all of us and the hopefulness and support he has afforded many in hours of gloom or trouble. Standing apart from criticism, the poem is brave, energetic, stimulant, and proves still true Browning's line of self-description in *Pauline*, self-description which no moment lived, no line written since has annulled, and which is the 'secret' of Browning's greatness—

"I am made up of an intensest life."

INDEX

ABT VOGLER, 126
Adam, Lilith, and Eve, 222
After, 117
Agamemnon of Æschylus, The, 202
Andrea del Sarto, 116
Another Way of Love, 123
Any Wife to any Husband, 111
Apollo and the Fates. A Prologue, 234
Apparent Failure, 131
Appearances, 200
Arcades Ambo, 243
Aristophanes' Apology, 182
Artemis Prologizes, 82
Asolando, 239
At the "Mermaid," 198
Avison, Charles, Parleying with, 238

BAD DREAMS, 242
Balaustion's Adventure; including A Transcript from Euripides, 161
Baldinucci, Filippo, on the Privilege of Burial, 202
Bartoli, Daniel, Parleying with, 235
Bean-Feast, The, 243
Bean-Stripe, A: also Apple-Eating, 231
Beatrice Signorini, 244
Before, 117
Bells and Pomegranates, 75-103
Bifurcation, 199
Bishop Blougram's Apology, 115
Bishop, The, orders his Tomb at Saint Praxed's Church, 93
Blot in the 'Scutcheon, A, 86
Book, The, and the Ring, 160
Boot and Saddle, 81
Boy, The, and the Angel, 95
By the Fireside, 111

CALIBAN UPON SETEBOS, 128
Camel-Driver, A, 229
Caponsacchi, Giuseppe, 148
Cardinal, The, and the Dog, 243
Cavalier Tunes, 81
Cenciaja, 201
Cherries, 230
"Childe Roland to the Dark Tower came," 113

Christmas-Eve, 103
Cleon, 121
Clive, 217
Colombe's Birthday, 88
Confessional, The, 94
Confessions, 129
Count Gismond, 81
Count Guido Franceschini, 146
Cristina, 82
Cristina and Monaldeschi, 221

"DE GUSTIBUS ——," 120
Deaf and Dumb; a Group by Woolner, 129
Death in the Desert, A, 127
Development, 245
De Lairesse, Gerard, Parleying with, 237
De Mandeville, Bernard, Parleying with, 234
Dîs Aliter Visum; or, le Byron de nos Jours, 126
Doctor ——, 219
Dodington, George Bubb, Parleying with, 236
Dominus Hyacinthus de Archangelis, 152
Donald, 220
Dramatic Idyls, First Series, 211
Dramatic Idyls, Second Series, 217
Dramatic Lyrics, 81
Dramatic Romances and Lyrics, 92
Dramatis Personæ, 124
Dubiety, 241

EAGLE, THE, 227
Earth's Immortalities, 95
Easter-Day, 105
Echetlos, 217
Englishman, The, in Italy, 92
Epilogue to Asolando, 245
Epilogue to Dramatis Personæ, 131
Epilogue to Ferishtah's Fancies, 232
Epilogue to Pacchiarotto, 202
Epistle, An, containing the Strange Medical Experience of Karshish, the Arab Physician, 111
Eurydice to Orpheus; a Picture by Leighton, 129
Evelyn Hope, 109

INDEX.

Face, A, 130
Family, The, 228
Fears and Scruples, 199
Ferishtah's Fancies, 226
Fifine at the Fair, 170
Flight of the Duchess, The, 94
Flower's Name, The, 94
Flute-music, with an Accompaniment, 244
Forgiveness, A, 200
Fra Lippo Lippi, 110
Furini, Francis, Parleying with, 236
Fust and his Friends: An Epilogue, 238

Garden Fancies, 94
Give a Rouse, 81
Glove, The, 97
Gold Hair: a Story of Pornic, 124
Grammarian's Funeral, A, 122
Guardian-Angel, The, 121
Guido, 157

Halbert and Hob, 214
Half-Rome, 141
Heretic's Tragedy, The, 122
Hervé Riel, 200
Holy-Cross Day, 121
Home-Thoughts, from Abroad, 93
Home-Thoughts, from the Sea, 93
House, 198
How it Strikes a Contemporary, 114
"How they brought the Good News from Ghent to Aix," 92
Humility, 241

"Imperante Augusto natus est ——" 244
In a Balcony, 118
In a Gondola, 82
In a Year, 118
In Three Days, 117
Inapprehensiveness, 243
Incident of the French Camp, 81
Inn Album, The, 188
Instans Tyrannus, 112
Italian, The, in England, 92
Iván Ivánovitch, 215
Ixion, 223

James Lee's Wife, 124
Jochanan Hakkadosh, 223
Jocoseria, 220
Johannes Agricola in Meditation, 83
Juris Doctor Johannes-Baptista Bottinius, 154

King Victor and King Charles, 78

La Saisiaz, 207
Laboratory, The, 94
Lady, The, and the Painter, 243
Last Ride Together, The, 115
Life in a Love, 114
Light Woman, A, 114
Likeness, A, 130
Lost Leader, The, 93
Lost Mistress, The, 93
Love among the Ruins, 108
Love in a Life, 114
Lover's Quarrel, A, 109
Luria, 97

Magical Nature, 199
Marching Along, 81
Martin Relph, 212
Mary Wollstonecraft and Fuseli, 222
Master Hugues of Saxe-Gotha, 115
May and Death, 129
Meeting at Night, 95
Melon-Seller, The, 227
Memorabilia, 116
Men and Women, 108
Mesmerism, 112
Mihrab Shah, 229
Misconceptions, 123
Mr. Sludge, "The Medium," 130
Muckle-Mouth Meg, 243
Muléykeh, 218
My Last Duchess, 81
My Star, 112

Nationality in Drinks, 95
Natural Magic, 199
Ned Bratts, 216
Never the Time and the Place, 226
Now, 241
Numpholeptos, 199

Old Pictures in Florence, 118
One Way of Love, 122
One Word More. To E. B. B., 123
Other Half-Rome, The, 143

Pacchiarotto and how he worked in Distemper: with other poems, 196
Pacchiarotto, Of, and how he worked in Distemper, 197
Pambo, 226
Pan and Luna, 219
Paracelsus, 53
Parleyings with Certain People of Importance in their Day, 233

Parting at Morning, 95
Patriot, The, 115
Pauline; A Fragment of a Confession, 49
Pearl, A, A Girl, 242
Pheidippides, 213
Pictor Ignotus, 92
Pied Piper of Hamelin, The,—A Child's Story, 83
Pietro of Abano, 218
Pillar at Sebzevar, A, 231
Pippa Passes, 75
Pisgah Sights, 198
Plot-Culture, 231
Poetics, 241
Pompilia, 150
Ponte dell' Angelo, Venice, 244
Pope, The, 155
Pope, The, and the Net, 243
Popularity, 122
Porphyria's Lover, 83
Pretty Woman, A, 113
Prince Hohenstiel - Schwangau, Saviour of Society, 166
Prologue to Asolando, 240
Prologue to Ferishtah's Fancies, 227
Prologue to Pacchiarotto, 197
Prospice, 129
Protus, 120

RABBI BEN EZRA, 127
Red Cotton Night-Cap Country, or Turf and Towers, 177
Rephan, 245
Respectability, 113
Return, The, of the Druses, 83
Reverie, 245
Ring, The, and the Book, 131
Rosny, 240
Rudel to the Lady of Tripoli, 82

SAUL, 96

Serenade, A, at the Villa, 112
Shah Abbas, 228
Shop, 198
Sibrandus Schafnaburgensis, 94
Smart, Christopher, Parleying with, 235
Soliloquy of the Spanish Cloister, 81
Solomon and Balkis, 221
Song, 95
Sordello, 64
Soul's Tragedy, A, 101
Speculative, 242
Statue, The, and the Bust, 114
St. Martin's Summer, 200
Strafford, 61
Summum Bonum, 241
Sun, The, 228

TERTIUM QUID, 145
Through the Metidja to Abd-el-Kadr, 83
Time's Revenges, 96
Toccata of Galuppi's, A, 110
Too Late, 126
"Transcendentalism," 123
Tray, 216
Twins, The, 121
Two Camels, 230
Two in the Campagna, 122
Two Poets of Croisic, The, 210

UP AT A VILLA—DOWN IN THE CITY, 109

WARING, 82
Which? 243
White Witchcraft, 242
Woman's Last Word, A, 109
Women and Roses, 120
Worst of It, The, 125

YOUTH AND ART, 130

THE END.